Reasoning Olympiad

Highly useful for all school students participating
in Various Olympiads & Competitions

Series Editor Keshav Mohan
Author Shweta Chaturvedi

Class 1

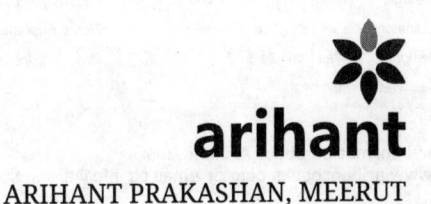

arihant
ARIHANT PRAKASHAN, MEERUT

ARIHANT PRAKASHAN, MEERUT
All Rights Reserved

© Publisher
No part of this publication may be re-produced, stored in a retrieval system or distributed in any form or by any means, electronic, mechanical, photocopying, recording, scanning, web or otherwise without the written permission of the publisher. Arihant has obtained all the information in this book from the sources believed to be reliable and true. However, Arihant or its editors or authors or illustrators don't take any responsibility for the absolute accuracy of any information published, and the damages or loss suffered thereupon.

Administrative & Production Offices

Regd. Office 'Ramchhaya' 4577/15, Agarwal Road, Darya Ganj New Delhi -110002
Tele: 011- 47630600, 43518550; Fax: 011- 23280316

Head Office Kalindi, TP Nagar, Meerut (UP) - 250002
Tele: 0121-2401479, 2512970, 4004199; Fax: 0121-2401648
All disputes subject to Meerut (UP) jurisdiction only.

Sales & Support Offices
Agra, Ahmedabad, Bengaluru, Bhubaneswar, Bareilly, Chennai, Delhi, Guwahati, Haldwani, Hyderabad, Jaipur, Jhansi, Kolkata, Kota, Lucknow, Meerut, Nagpur & Pune

ISBN 978-93-5094-413-4

Price ₹50.00

Typeset by Arihant DTP Unit at Meerut
Printed & Bound by Arihant Publications (I) Ltd. (Press Unit)

Production Team
Publishing Manager	Amit Verma	Page Layouting	Ravi Saini & Shravan Pandey
Project Coordinator	Shelly Singhal	Figure Illustrator	Brahampal Singh & Shanker Rajput
Cover Designer	Syed Darin Zaidi	Proof Reader	Rachi Aggarwal
Inner Designer	Ravi Negi		

For further information about Arihant Books
log on to www.arihantbooks.com or email to info@arihantbooks.com

Preface

Reasoning Olympiad Series for Class 1st-10th is a series of books, which will challenge the young inquisitive minds by the non-routine and exciting Reasoning or Logic based problems.

The main purpose of this series is to make the students ready for competitive exams, as Reasoning is an integral section of almost all competitive examinations. All the questions given in this series are objective in nature so, they will provide students a feel of competitive examinations as school/board exams are of qualifying nature, but not competitive, which mainly have Objective Questions.

- **Need of Olympiad Series**
  This series helps students, who are willing to sharpen their problem solving skills through logical thinking. Unlike typical assessment books, which emphasise on drilling practice, the focus of this series is on practising problem solving techniques.

- **Development of Logical Approach**
  The thought provoking questions given in this series will help students to attain a deeper understanding of the concepts and through, which students will be able to imbibe reasoning/Logical/Analytical skills in themselves.

- **Complement Your School Studies**
  This series complements the additional preparation needs of students for regular school/board exams. As most of the schools conduct aptitude test on a regular basis. Along with, it will also address all the requirements of the students, who are approaching National/State level competitions or Olympiads.

I shall welcome criticism from the students, teachers, educators and parents. I would also like to hear from all of you about errors and short comings, which may have remained in this edition and the suggestions for their improvement in the next edition.

Editor

Content

1.	Matching Pairs	1-6
2.	Which One is Different?	7-9
3.	What Comes Next?	10-14
4.	Similar Shapes and Grouping of Figures	15-18
5.	Hidden Shapes and Pattern Completion	19-24
6.	Ranking Test	25-30

Practice Sets — 31-40

Answers and Explanations — 41-44

1

Matching Pairs

Let us Learn

Direction (Ex. Nos. 1-2) Complete the second pair in the same way as the first pair.

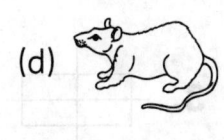

Example 1 🐱 : 🐄 :: 🐦 : ?

(a) tiger (b) goat (c) parrot (d) rat

Explanation. *(c)* As cat and cow are animals. Similarly, crow and parrot are birds.

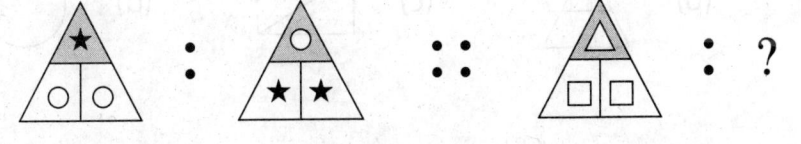

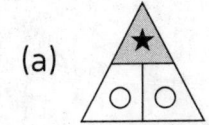

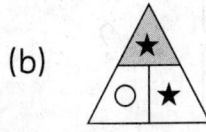

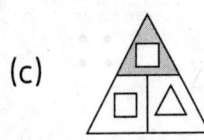

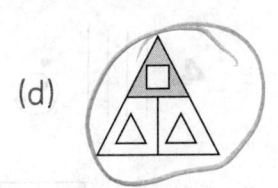

Example 2

Explanation. *(d)* In the first pair, ★ is replaced by ○ and ○ is replaced by ★. Similarly, in the second pair, △ is replaced by □ and □ is replaced by △.

Let's Practice

Direction (Q. Nos. 1-24) Their is a certain relationship between the pair of figures given on either side of (::). Identify the relationship of given pair and find the matching term.

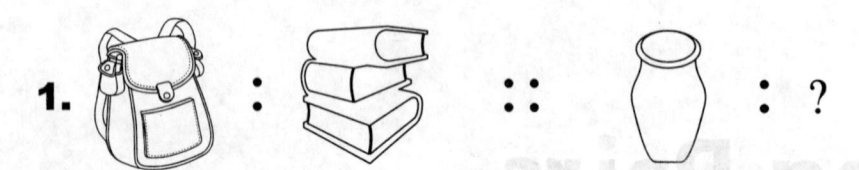

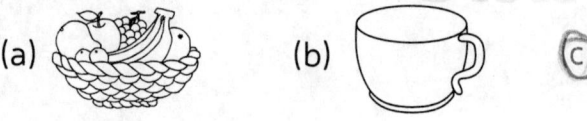

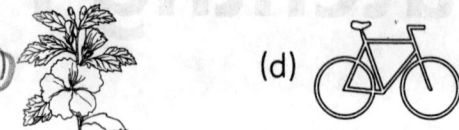

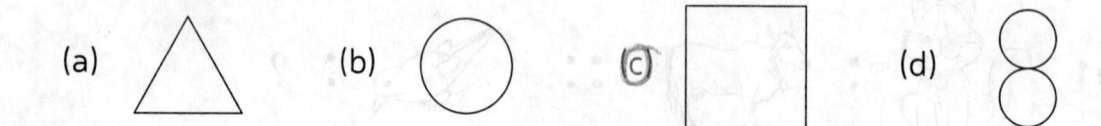

1. [bag] : [books] :: [vase] : ?

   (a) [basket of fruits]   (b) [cup]   (c) [flower]   (d) [bicycle]

2. [4 dots] : [triangle] :: [5 dots] : ?

   (a) [triangle]   (b) [circle]   (c) [square]   (d) [two circles]

3. [rectangle with cross] : [rectangle] :: [hexagon with cross] : ?

   (a) [hexagon]   (b) [triangle with lines]   (c) [rectangle with diagonal]   (d) [circle]

4. [4 vertical lines] : [triangle] :: [3 curvy lines] : ?

   (a) [square]   (b) [star]   (c) [circle with line]   (d) [triangle]

2 Reasoning Olympiad Class I

5.  ⬡ : ⬡ :: ⬭ : ?

(a) 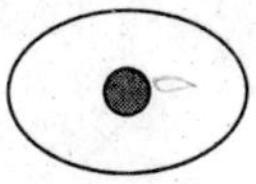 ⬭ (b) 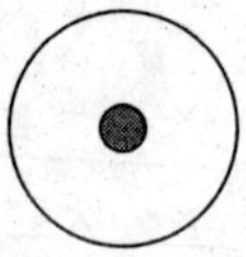 ◯ (c)  ⬤ (d) 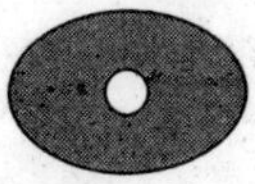 ⬭

6. $\frac{X}{B}$: BX :: $\frac{M}{C}$: ?

(a) XC
(b) MA
(c) XC
(d) CM

7. 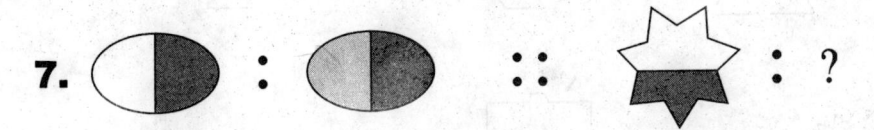 ⬭ : ⬭ :: ★ : ?

(a)  (b)  (c)  (d)

8. 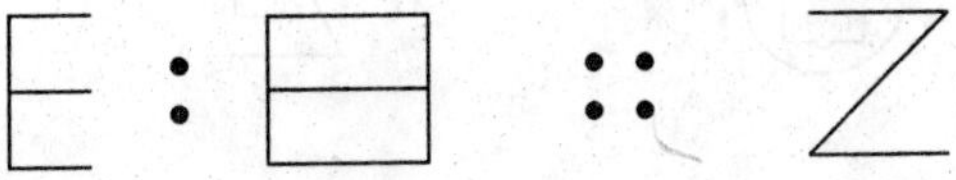 ⊟ : ⊟ :: Z : ?

(a)  ▭ (b)  } (c)  ⊠ (d) 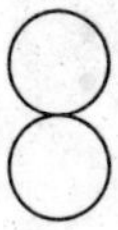 8

9. 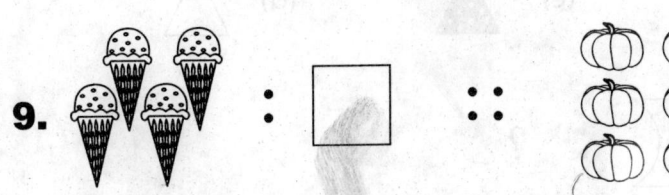 🍦 : ▢ :: 🎃 : ?

(a)  △ (b) ◯ (c) 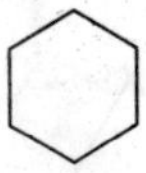 ⬡ (d) 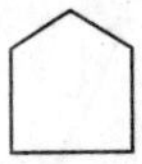 ⌂

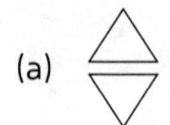

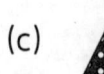

10.  ÷×÷ : ÷÷÷ :: ×|× : ?

(a)  ×××× (b) ×·× (c)  ×× × (d) 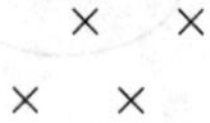 × ×

11. 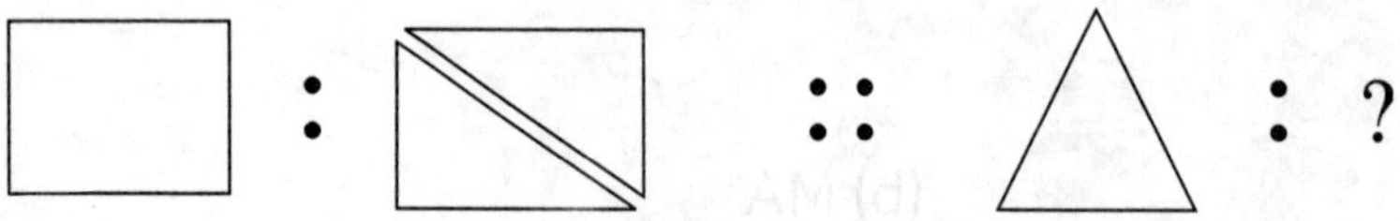 □ : ▨ :: △ : ?

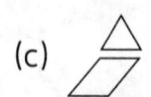

(a) ▲▽ (b) ⌂ (c) ◿ (d)  ◨

12. 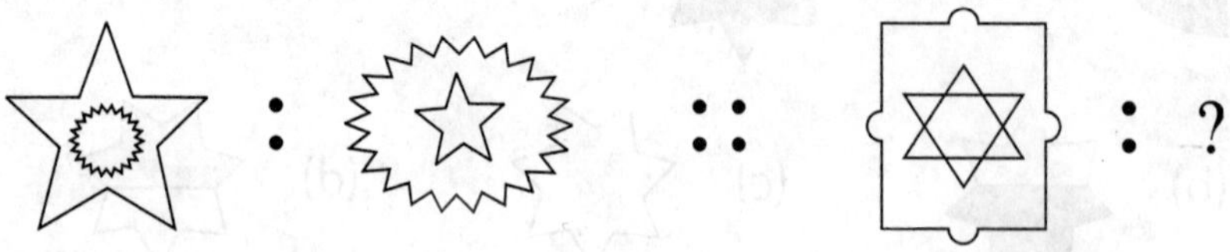 ★ : ✦ :: ✡ : ?

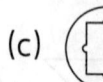

(a) 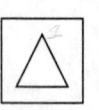 □△ (b)  ✡ (c)  ◯ (d) 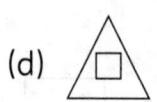 △□

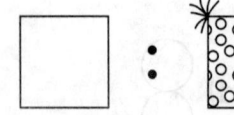

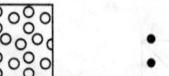

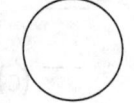

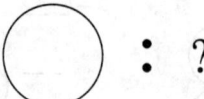

13. □ : ▦ :: ◯ : ?

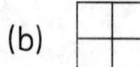

(a)  ⚽ (b) ⊞ (c)  🎉 (d)  △

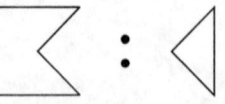

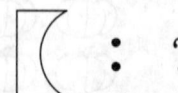

14. ⊲ : ◁ :: ⊃ : ?

(a)  ◗ (b) 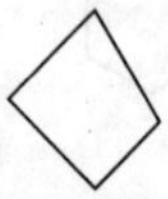 ◇ (c) 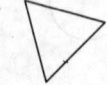 ▽ (d)  ⋈

Reasoning Olympiad Class I

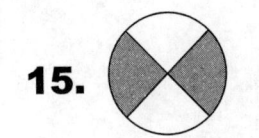

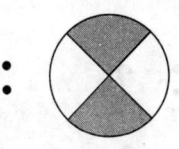

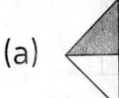

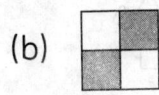

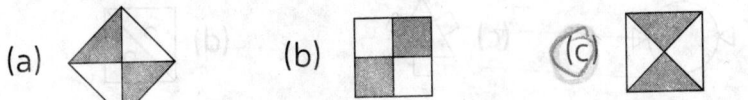

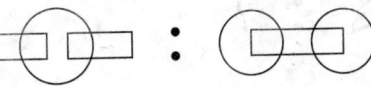

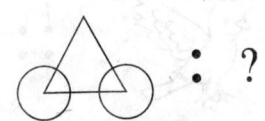

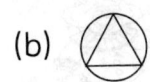

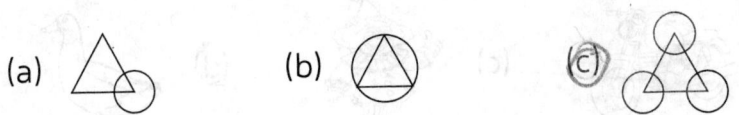

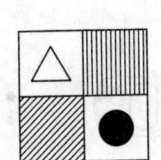

15. 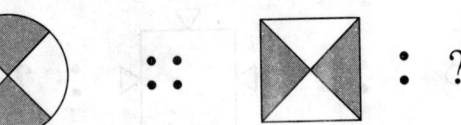 ◯ : ◯ :: ◻ : ?

(a) 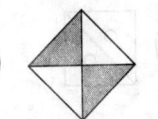   (b)   (c)   (d)

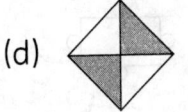

16. : :: : ?

(a) 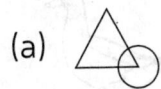   (b)   (c)   (d)

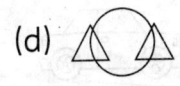

17. 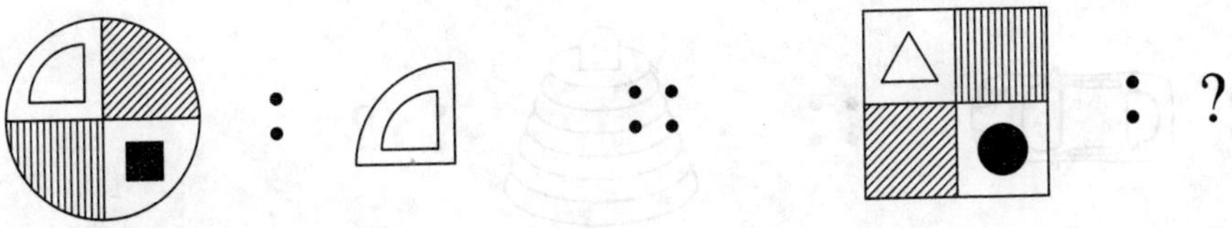 : :: : ?

(a) 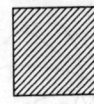   (b)    (c) 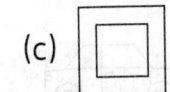   (d)

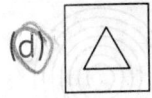

18. 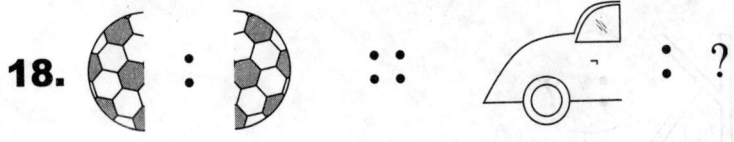 : :: : ?

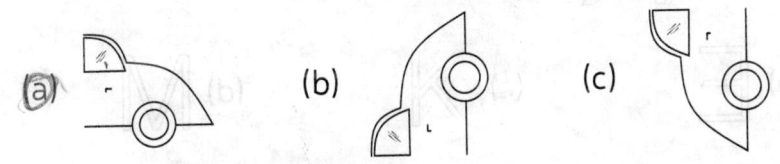

(a)   (b) 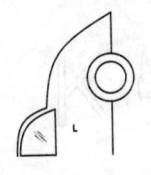   (c) 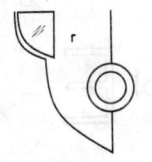   (d)

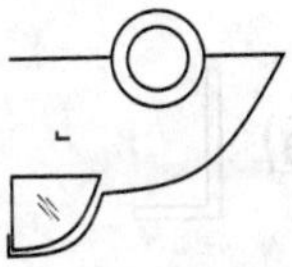

19. 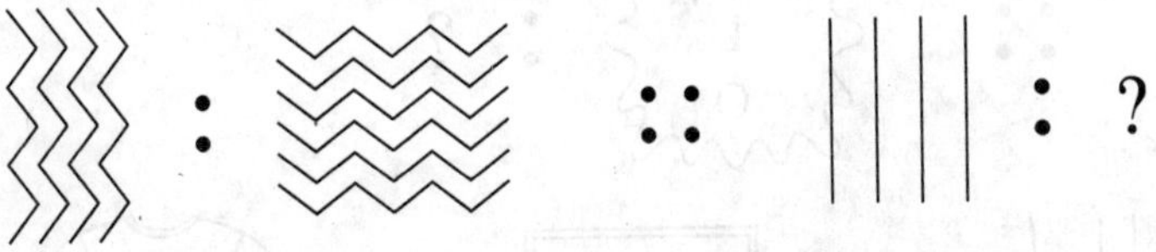 : :: : ?

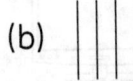

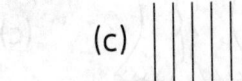

(a) 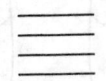   (b)   (c)   (d)

Matching Pairs 5

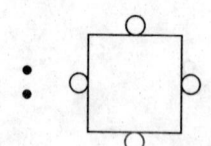

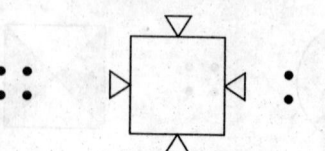

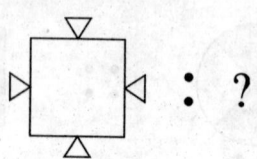

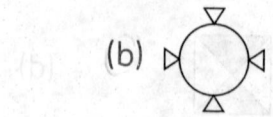

20. 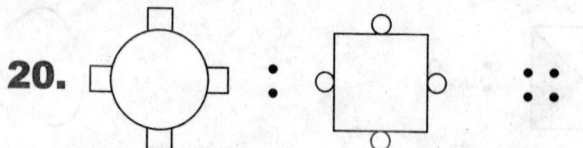 ○ : □ :: ▽□▷ : ?
   (a) 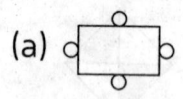 □   (b) ○   (c) 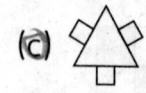 △   (d) 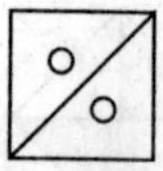 ◻

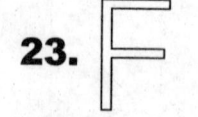

21. ✈ : 🐦 :: 🚢 : ?
   (a) 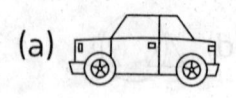 car   (b)  motorcycle   (c)  clown   (d)  duck

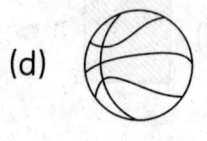

22. 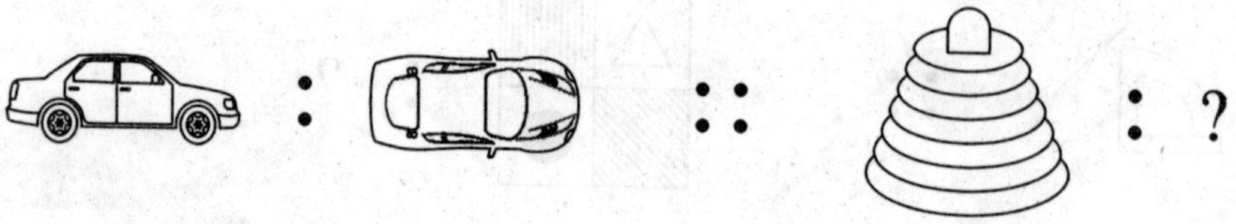 car : car(top view) :: pyramid : ?
   (a) 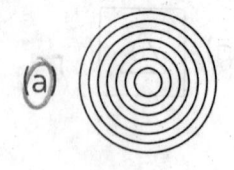 circles   (b) car   (c) doll   (d) basketball

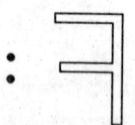

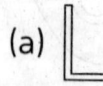

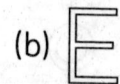

23. 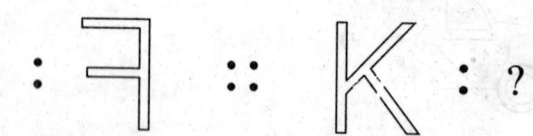 F : ꟻ :: K : ?
   (a) L   (b) E   (c)  ꓘ   (d)  M

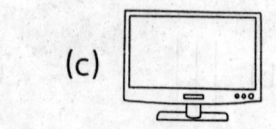

24.  D K C U : duck :: I N L O : ?
   (a)  tiger   (b) 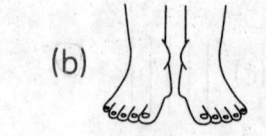 feet   (c) TV   (d) T-shirt

6 Reasoning Olympiad Class I

2

Which One is Different?

Let us Learn

Direction (Ex. Nos. 1-3) Which one is different from others?

Example 1 (a) 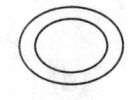 ⬭ (b) 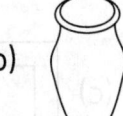 🏺 (c)  🫖 (d)  🥛

Explanation. *(a)* Except option (a), all are used to contain water or liquid.

Example 2 (a)  ◻ (b)  ◻ (c) 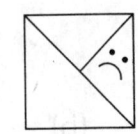 ◻ (d)  ◻

Explanation. *(c)* Except option (c), all design show smily face.

Example 3 (a)  ▽ (b)  ▽ (c) 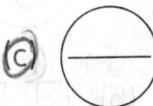 ⊖ (d)  ◻

Explanation. *(c)* In figures (a), (b) and (d), the number of sides of outer figure is equal to the number of lines present in it. Hence, option (c) is different from others.

Let's Practice

Direction (Q.Nos. 1-20) Find the odd one out from the given options.

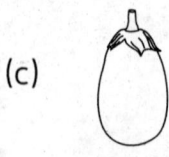

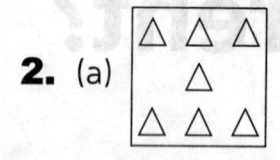

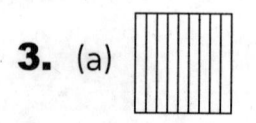

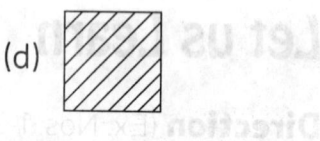

1. (a) grapes (b) 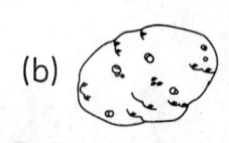 potato (c) brinjal (d)  ladyfinger

2. (a) square with 6 triangles (b) 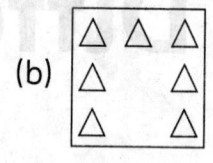 square with 6 triangles (c) 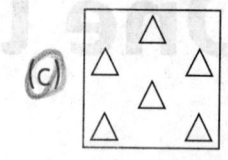 square with 5 triangles (d) 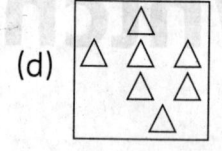 square with 6 triangles

3. (a) vertical lines (b) 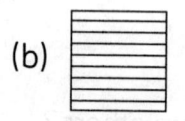 horizontal lines (c) 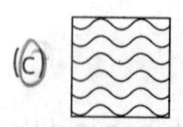 wavy lines (d) diagonal lines

4. (a) January   (b) March   (c) May   (d) April

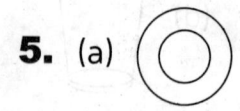

5. (a) circle in circle   (b)  triangle in triangle   (c) 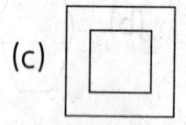 square   (d) 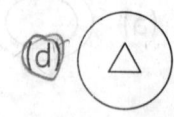 triangle in circle

6. (a)  ↑   (b)  →   (c)  ←   (d) 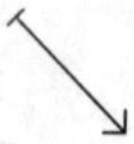 ↘

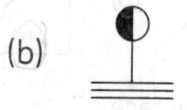

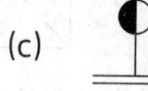

7. (a) 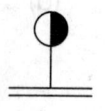   (b)   (c)   (d)

8. (a)    (b) 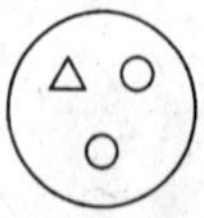   (c)    (d)

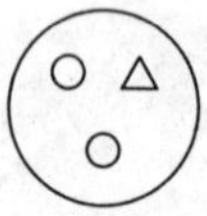

9. (a) 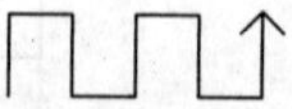   (b) 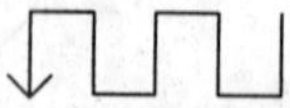   (c) 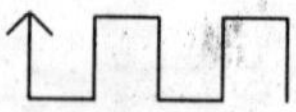   (d)

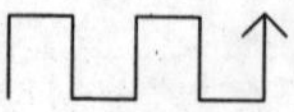

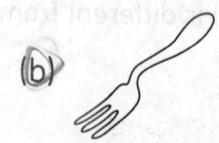

10. (a)  scissors   (b) fork   (c)  knife   (d) 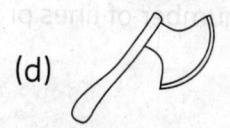 axe

8 Reasoning Olympiad Class I

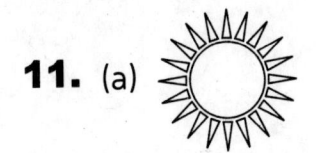

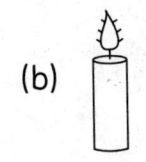

11. (a) sun (b) candle (c) bulb (d) 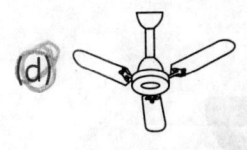 fan

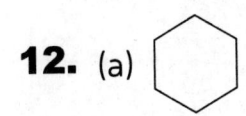

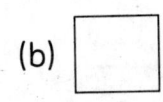

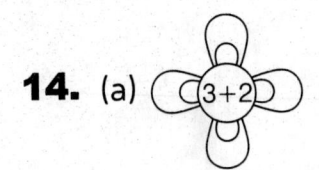

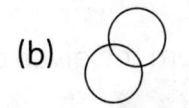

12. (a) hexagon (b) square (c) 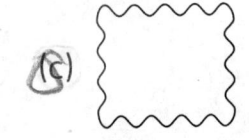 wavy square (d) 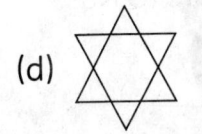 star

13. (a) (b) (c) (d)

14. (a) 3+2 (b) 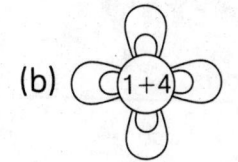 1+4 (c) 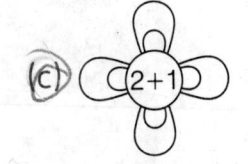 2+1 (d) 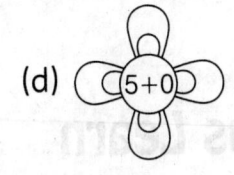 5+0

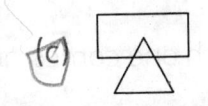

15. (a) 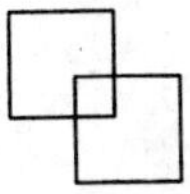 (b) (c) (d)

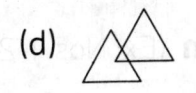

16. (a) 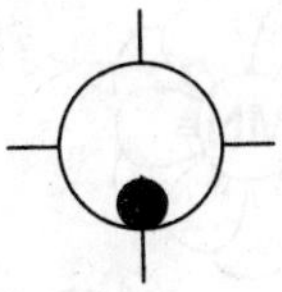 (b) 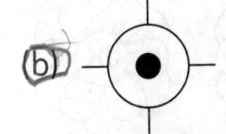 (c) 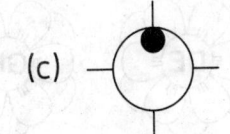 (d)

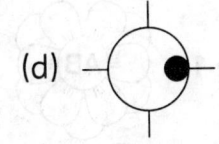

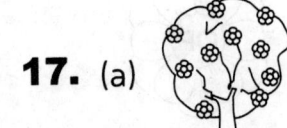

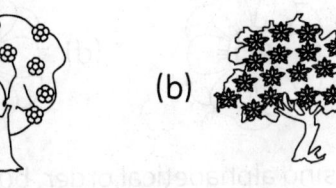

17. (a) (b) (c)  (d)

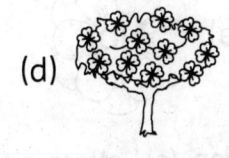

18. (a)  (b) 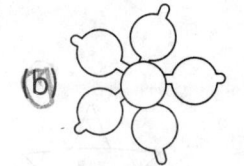 (c)  (d)

19. (a)  (b) 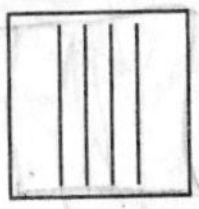 (c) 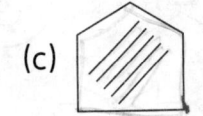 (d)

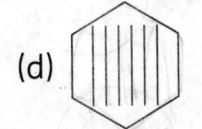

20. (a) 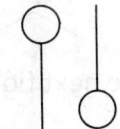 (b) 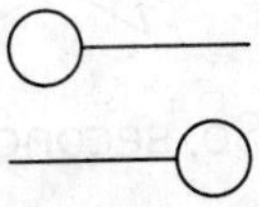 (c) 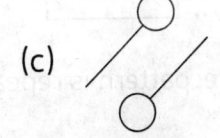 (d)

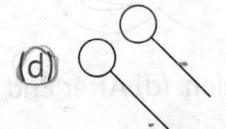

Which One is Different? 9

3

What Comes Next?

Let us Learn

Direction (Ex. Nos. 1-2) Which one comes next from the given options?

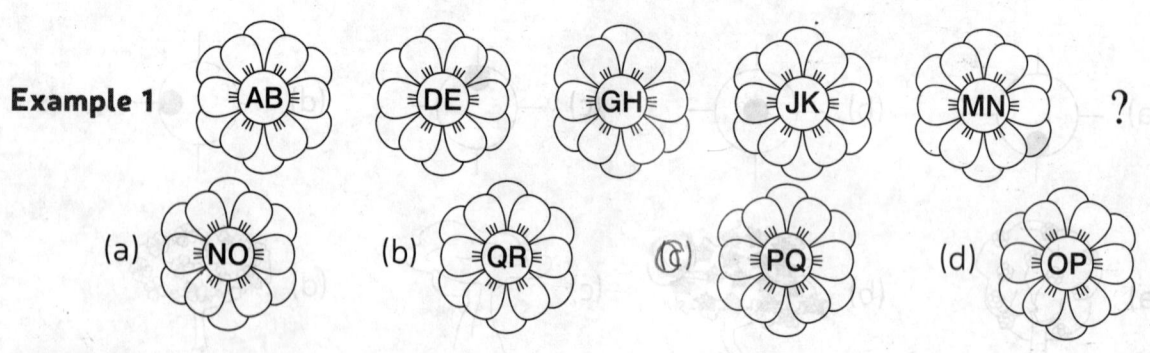

Example 1 AB DE GH JK MN ?

(a) NO (b) QR (c) PQ (d) OP

Explanation. *(c)* Letters in flower are arranged in increasing alphabetical order, but one letter is skipped in between the two flowers.

Example 2

(a) (b) (c) (d)

Explanation. *(d)* After 2nd figure, pattern is repeated. So, second figure will be next figure.

Let's Practice

Direction (Q. Nos. 1-17) Which figure/pattern/shape comes next?

1.

(a)   (b)   (c) □   (d) |

2.

(a)   (b)   (c)   (d)

3.

(a)   (b)   (c)   (d)

4.

(a) T   (b) U   (c) P   (d) V

What Comes Next?

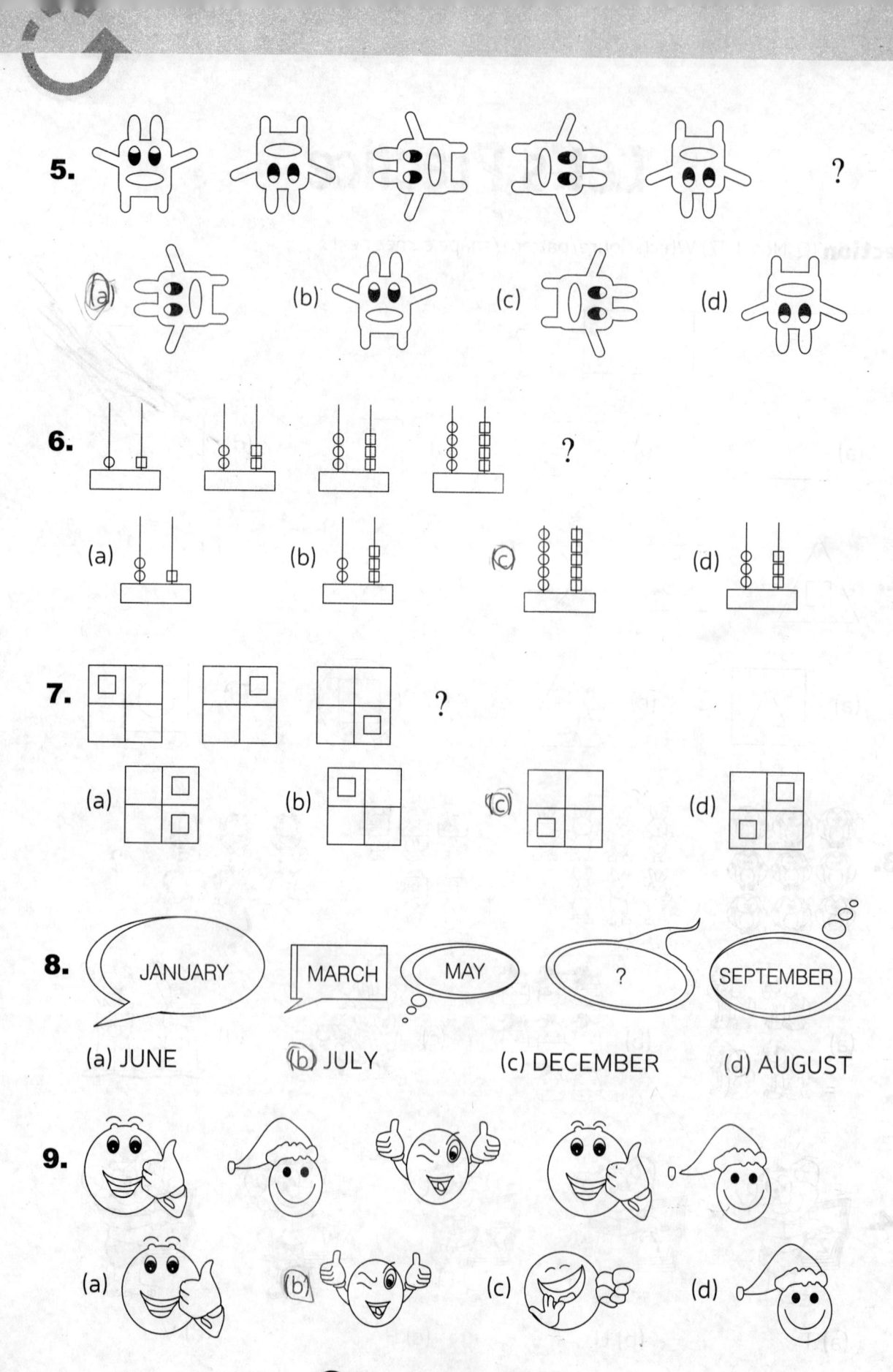

5.

(a) (b) (c) (d)

6.

(a) (b) (c) (d)

7.

(a) (b) (c) (d)

8. JANUARY   MARCH   MAY   ?   SEPTEMBER

(a) JUNE   (b) JULY   (c) DECEMBER   (d) AUGUST

9.

(a) (b) (c) (d)

12 Reasoning Olympiad Class I

10.

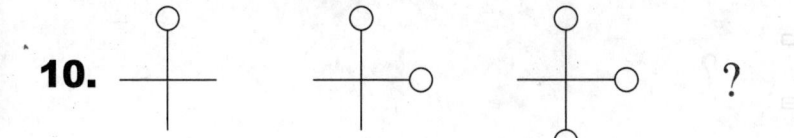

(a) 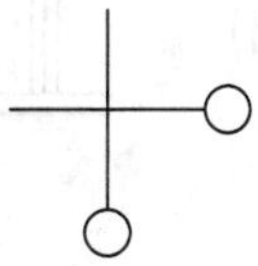   (b) 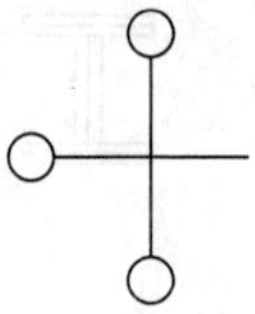   (c) 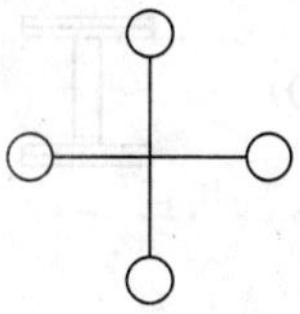   (d)

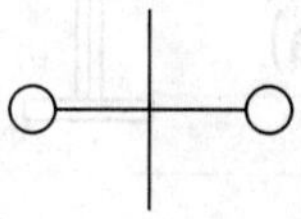

11.

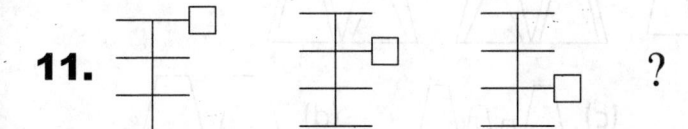

(a) 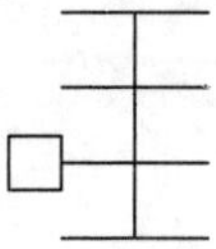   (b) 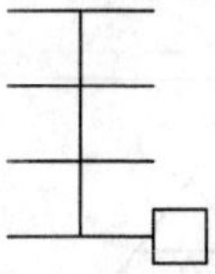   (c) 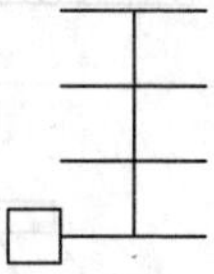   (d)

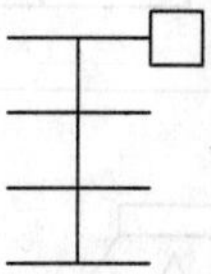

12.

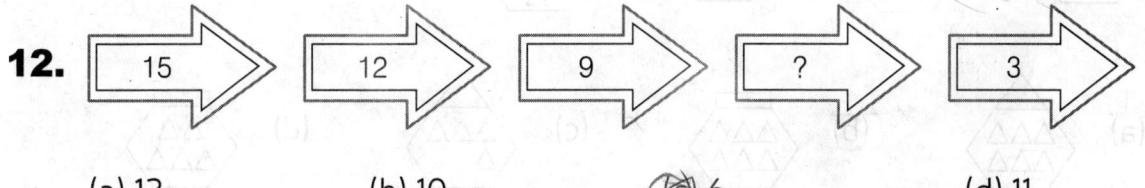

(a) 13   (b) 10   (c) 6   (d) 11

13.

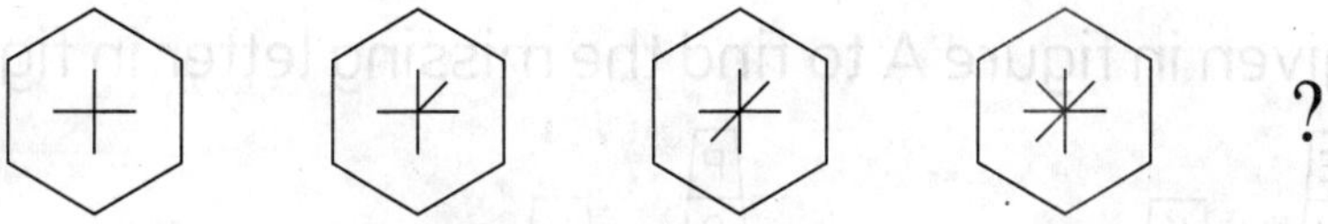

(a)    (b) 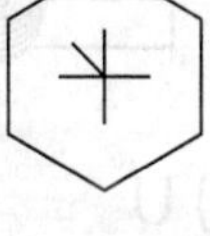   (c) 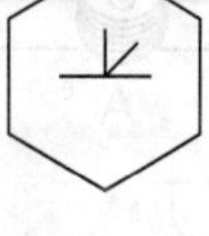   (d)

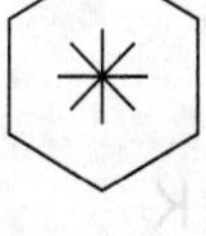

14.

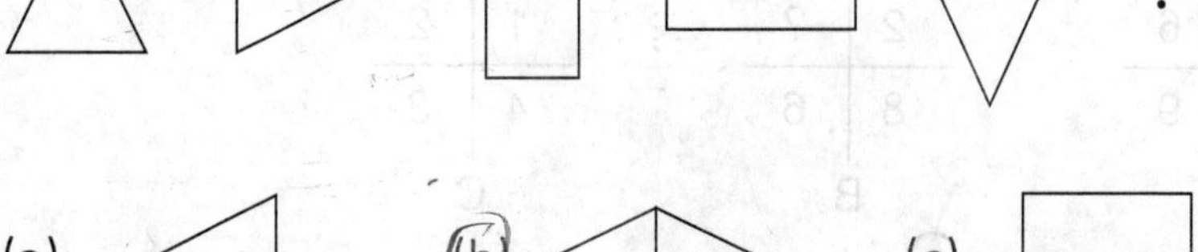

(a)   (b) 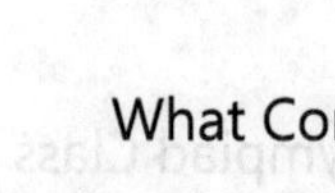   (c)    (d)

What Comes Next? 13

15. [figure] ?

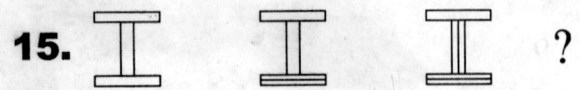

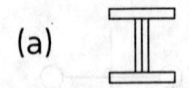

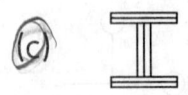

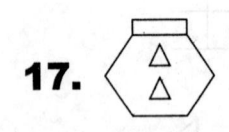

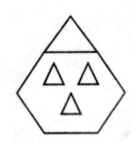

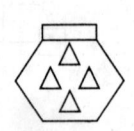

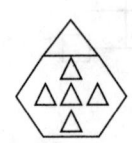

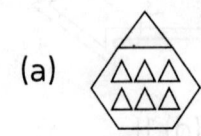

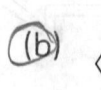

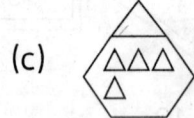

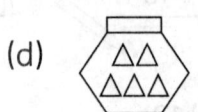

(a) [figure]   (b) [figure]   (c) [figure]   (d) [figure]

16. [figure] ?

(a) [figure]   (b) [figure]   (c) [figure]   (d) [figure]

17. [figure] ?

(a) [figure]   (b) [figure]   (c) [figure]   (d) [figure]

18. Follow the pattern given in figure A to find the missing letter in figure B.

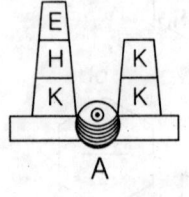

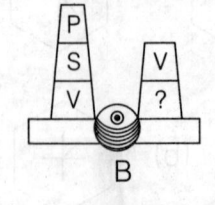

(a) K   (b) T   (c) U   (d) V

19. If same rule is followed in A, B and C, then find the missing number.

3	6
12	9

A

2	?
8	6

B

1	2
4	3

C

(a) 3   (b) 4   (c) 5   (d) 10

4

Similar Shapes and Grouping of Figures

Let us Learn

Example 1 Which object is exactly same as the given figure?

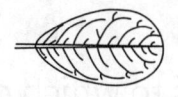

(a)  (b)  (c)  (d)

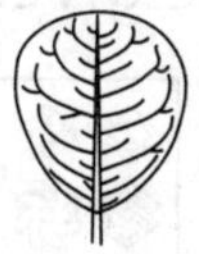

Explanation. *(d)* Option (d) is exactly same as question figure.

Example 2 Identify the object that belongs to the given group.

(a)  (b)  (c)  (d)

Explanation. *(d)* Letter 'B' is present in given group of letters. Hence, option (d) is correct.

Similar Shapes and Grouping of Figures

Let's Practice

Direction (Q. Nos. 1-3) Identify the object that belongs to the given group.

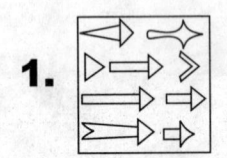

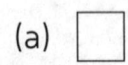

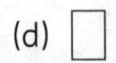

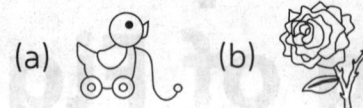

1. (a) □ (b) ○ (c) △ (d) ▭

2. (a) (b) (c) (d)

3. (a) (b) (c) (d)

4. The given figure ▯ belongs to which group.

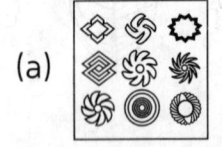

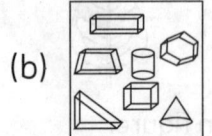

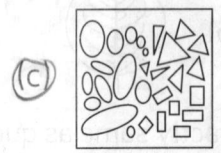

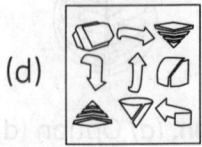

(a) (b) (c) (d)

Direction (Q. Nos. 5-16) Which object is same as the given figure?

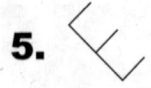

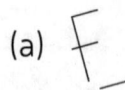

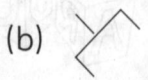

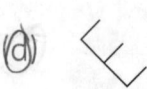

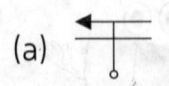

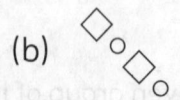

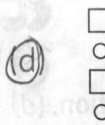

5. (a) (b) (c) (d)

6. (a) (b) (c) (d)

7. (a) □○□○ | (b) (c) (d)

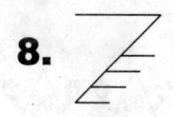

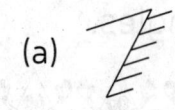

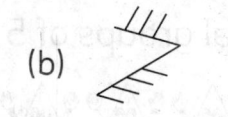

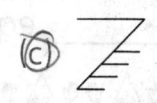

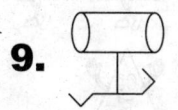

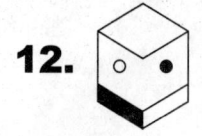

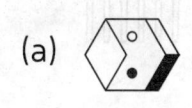

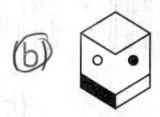

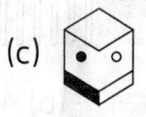

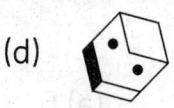

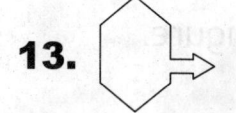

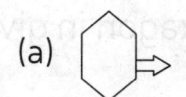

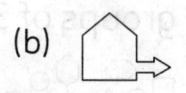

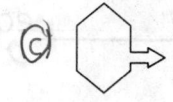

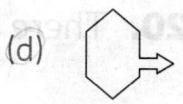

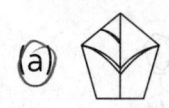

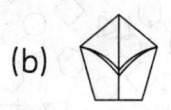

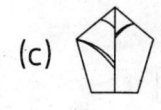

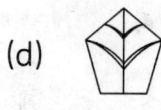

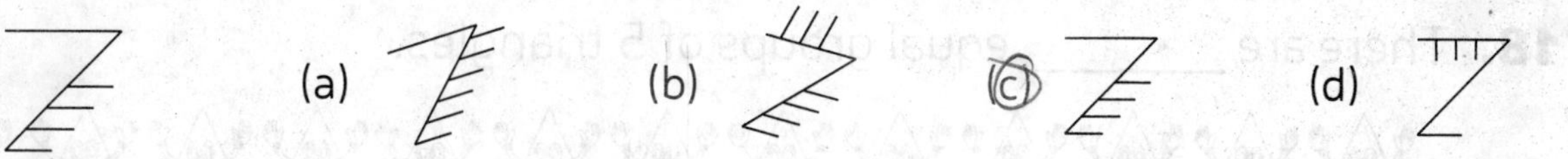

8. (a) (b) (c) (d)
9. 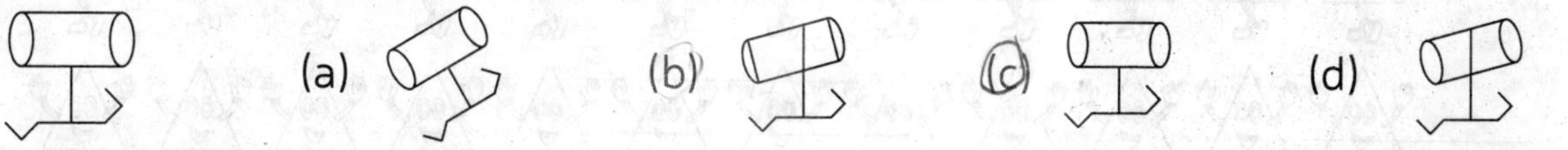 (a) (b) (c) (d)
10. 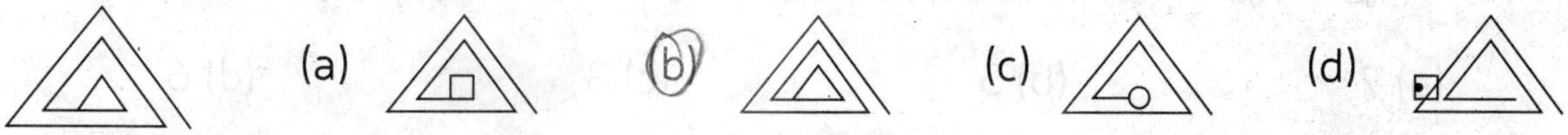 (a) (b) (c) (d)
11.  (a) (b) (c) (d)
12. (a) (b) (c) (d)
13. (a) (b) (c) (d)
14. (a) (b) (c) (d)
15. 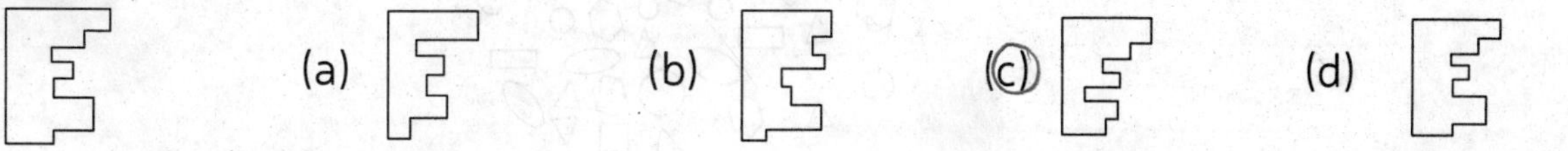 (a) (b) (c) (d)
16. 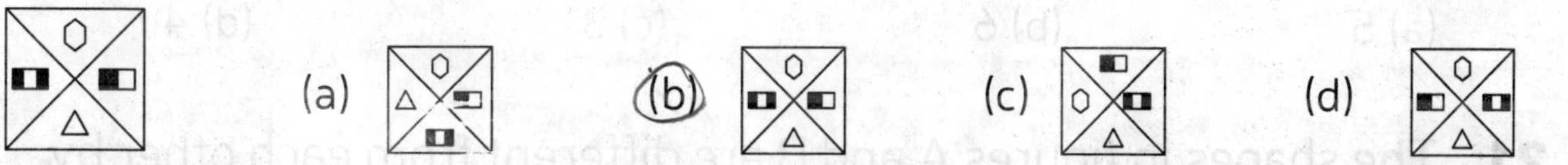 (a) (b) (c) (d)

17. There are _____ groups of 3 flowers.

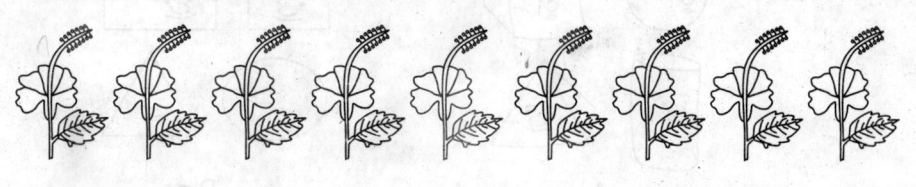

(a) 5   (b) 9   (c) 3   (d) 6

Similar Shapes and Grouping of Figures

18. There are _____ equal groups of 5 triangles.

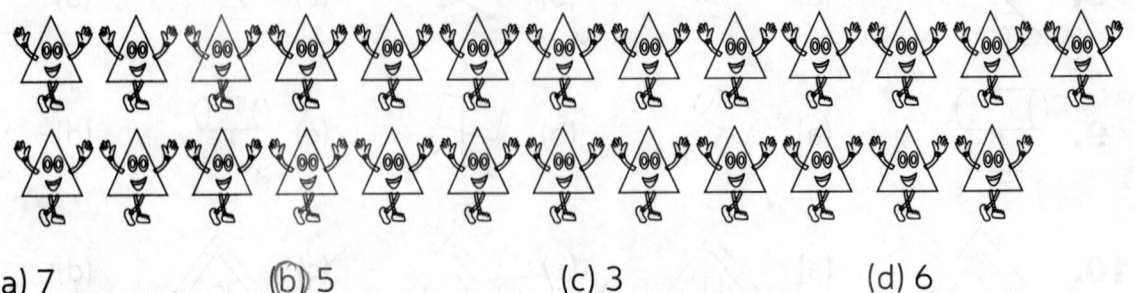

(a) 7   (b) 5   (c) 3   (d) 6

19. Number of the groups of 6 straws shown here is _____.

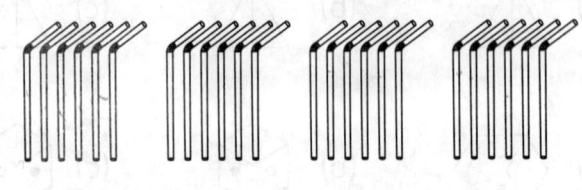

(a) 5   (b) 4   (c) 8   (d) 6

20. There are _____ equal groups of 3 hexagon in given figure.

(a) 5   (b) 6   (c) 3   (d) 4

21. The shapes in figures A and B are different from each other by _____.

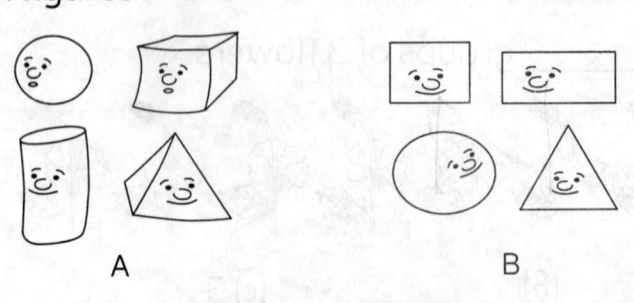

A   B

(a) shape   (b) size   (c) color   (d) shape and size

Reasoning Olympiad Class I

5

Hidden Shapes and Pattern Completion

Direction (Ex. Nos. 1-2) Observe the figure and answer the questions below it.

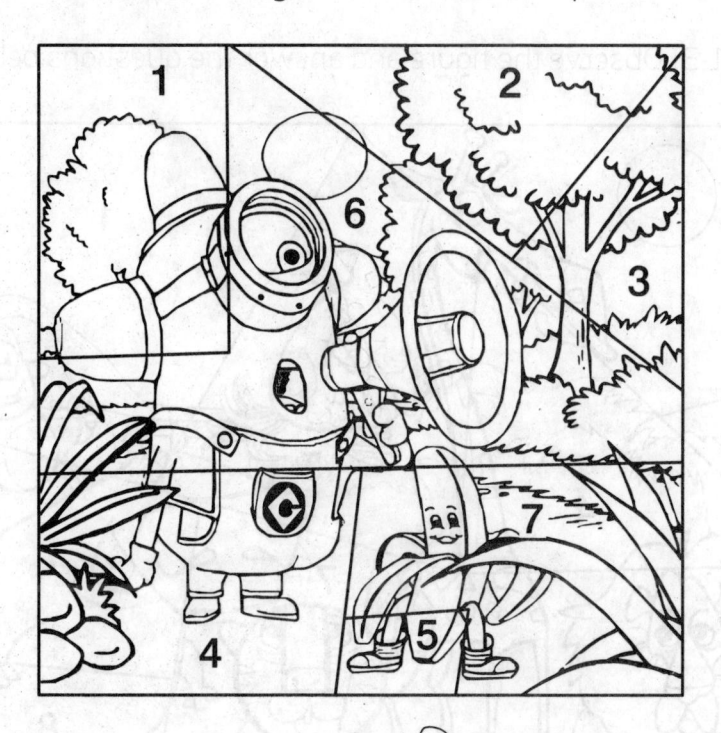

Example 1 In which part of the figure is the shape hidden?

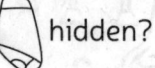

(a) 2   (b) 6   (c) 3   (d) 5

Explanation. *(b)* The shape given in the question is hidden in part 6.

Hidden Shapes and Pattern Completion   **19**

Example 2 Which shape is hidden in part 7?

(a)    (b)    (c)    (d)

Explanation. *(a)* Shape of option (a) is hidden in part 7.

Example 3 In which larger shape is the shape ⟡ hidden?

(a)   (b)   (c) 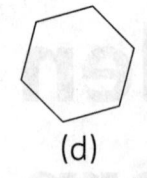   (d)

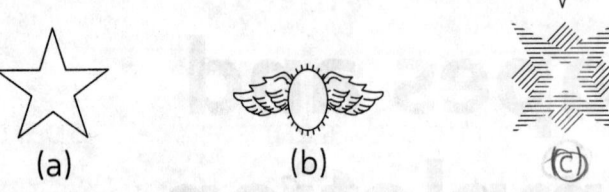

Explanation. *(c)* The given shape is hidden in option (c).

Let's Practice

Direction (Q. Nos. 1-3) Observe the figure and answer the questions below it.

1. Which shape is hidden in part 3?

(a)　　(b)　　(c)　　(d)

2. In which part of the figure is the shape hidden?

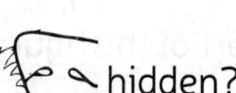

(a) 3　　(b) 7　　(c) 1　　(d) 5

3. How many of the pictures given in the box are hidden in the part 7?

(a) 4　　(b) 6　　(c) 1　　(d) 2

Direction (Q. Nos. 4-7) Observe the figure and answer the question below it.

Hidden Shapes and Pattern Completion 21

4. How many eyes are there in part 4?

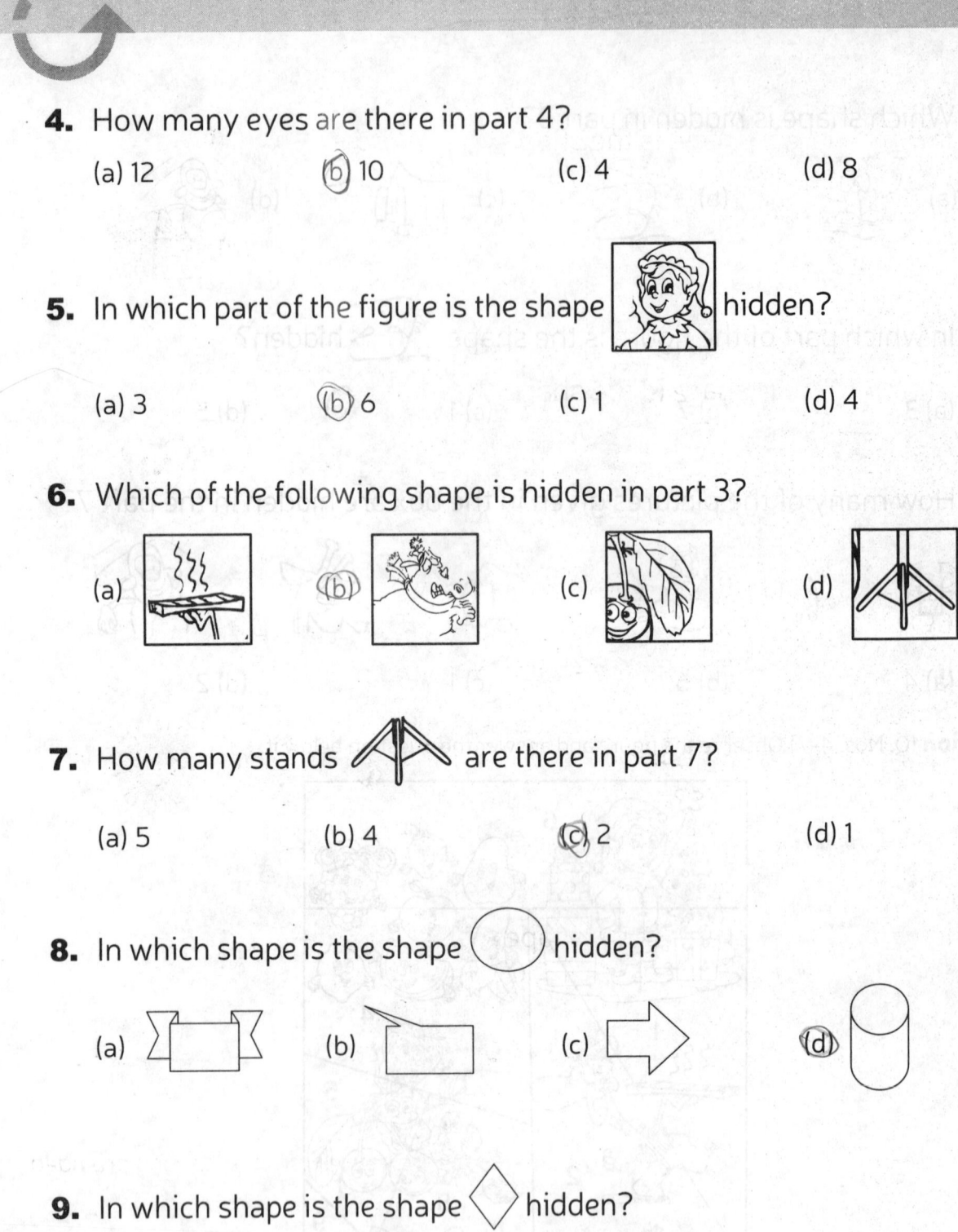

(a) 12 (b) 10 (c) 4 (d) 8

5. In which part of the figure is the shape [image] hidden?

(a) 3 (b) 6 (c) 1 (d) 4

6. Which of the following shape is hidden in part 3?

(a) (b) (c) (d)

7. How many stands [image] are there in part 7?

(a) 5 (b) 4 (c) 2 (d) 1

8. In which shape is the shape ◯ hidden?

(a) (b) (c) (d)

9. In which shape is the shape ◇ hidden?

(a) (b) (c) (d)

10. In which larger shape is the shape ⛰ hidden?

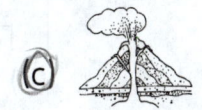

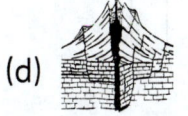

(a)   (b)   (c)   (d)

11. In which larger shape is the shape △ hidden?

(a)   (b)   (c)   (d)

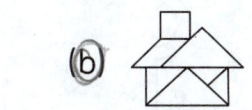

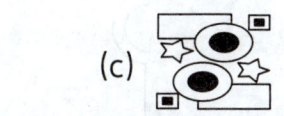

12. In which larger shape is the shape ◁ hidden?

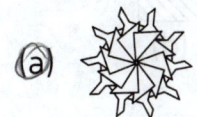

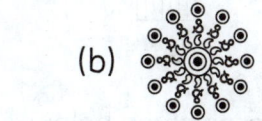

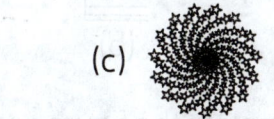

(a)   (b)   (c)   (d)

13. In which larger shape is the shape ▭ hidden?

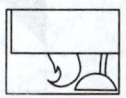

(a)   (b)   (c)   (d)

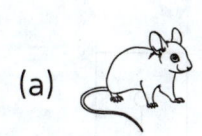

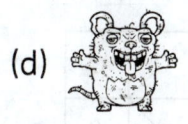

Direction (Q. Nos. 14-18) Find the other half of the given picture from the options provided.

14.

(a)   (b)   (c)   (d)

Hidden Shapes and Pattern Completion   23

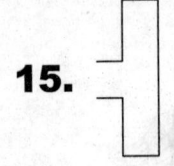

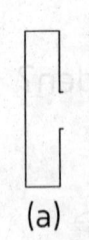

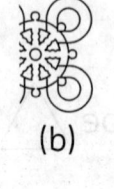

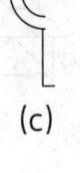

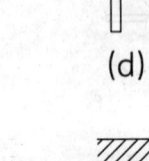

15.

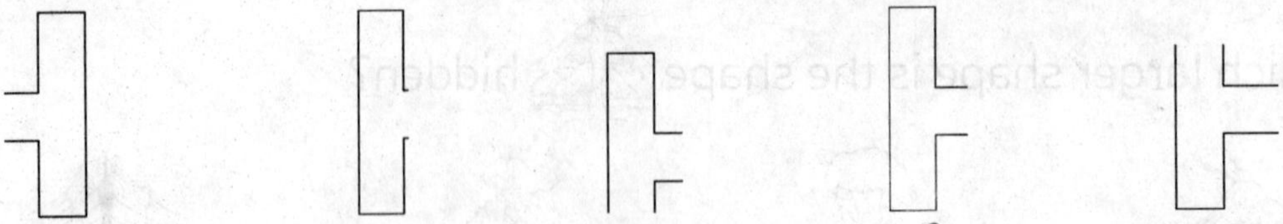

16.

17.

18.

Direction (Q. Nos. 19-22) Complete the figure patterns given below.

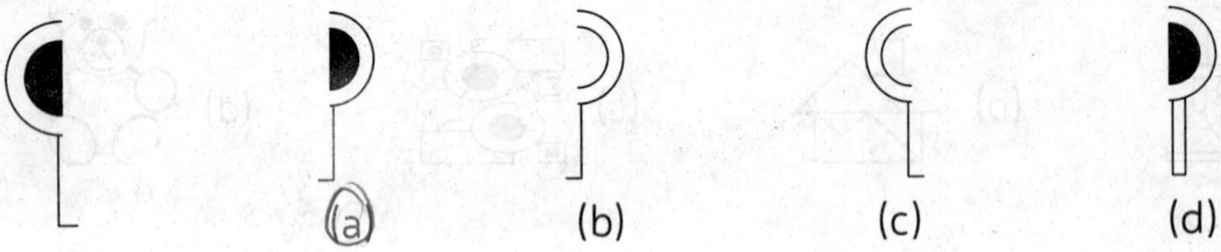

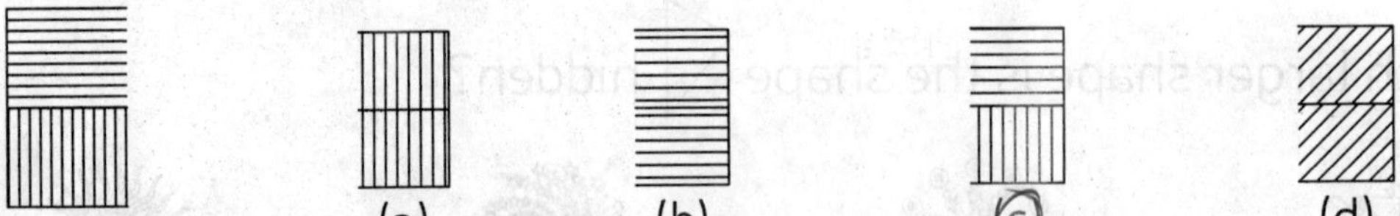

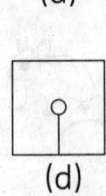

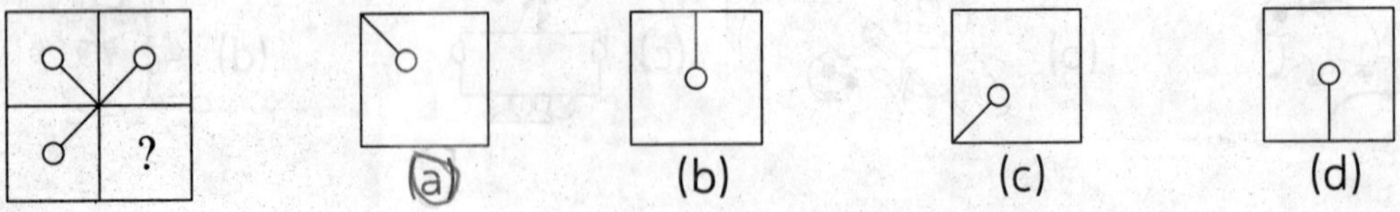

19.

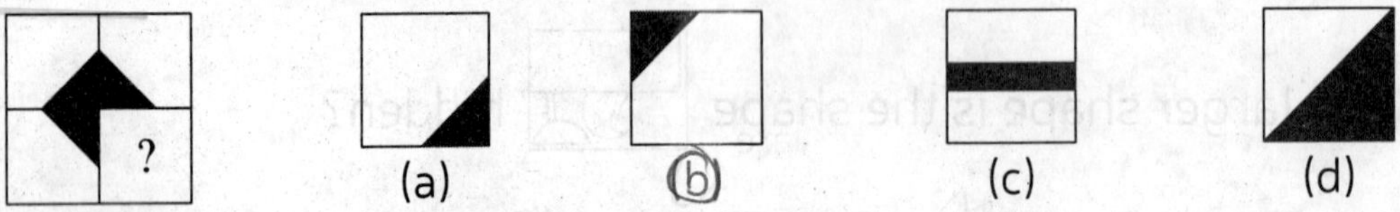

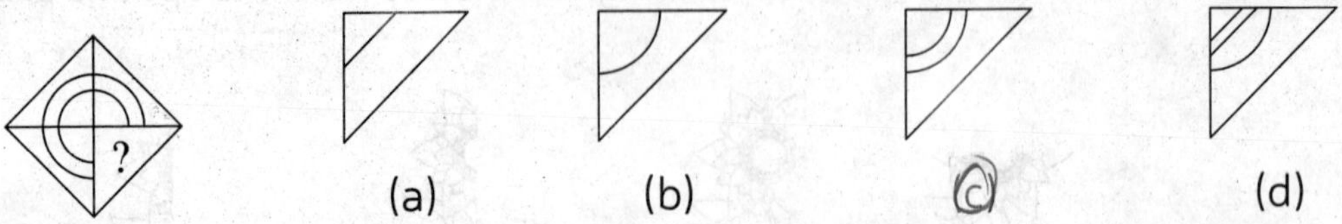

20.

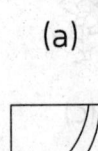

21.

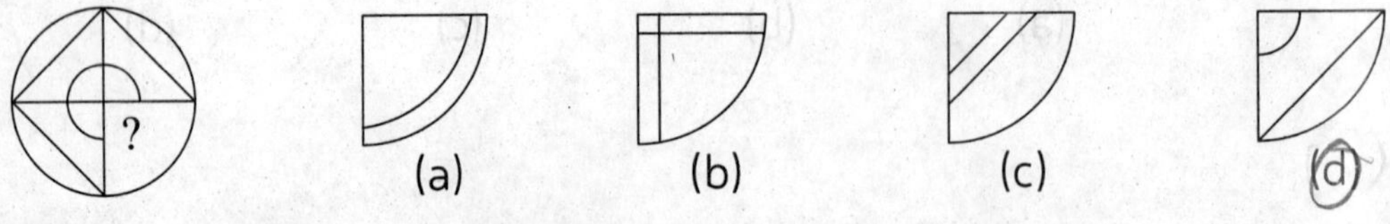

22.

6
Ranking Test

Let us Learn

Example 1. Which Sun is 5th from the right end?

P Q R S T U V W X

(a) U   (b) R   (c) T   (d) X

Explanation. *(c)* Sun T is fifth from right end.

Example 2. The position of the face in the square box is _____.

(a) 2nd from the right end
(b) 4th from the left end
(c) 3rd from the left end
(d) 4th from the right end

Explanation. *(d)* Face in square box is 4th from the right end.

Ranking Test 25

Let's Practice

1. Which monkey is fifth from the left end?

F K T P A O G I Z

(a) E   (b) H   (c) A   (d) F

2. Which image is 3rd from the right end?

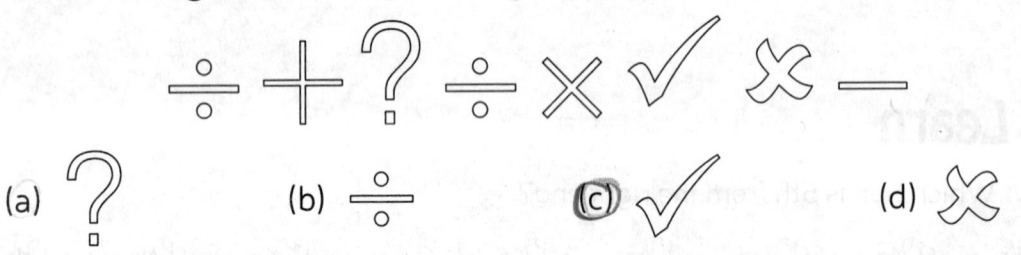

÷ + ? ÷ × ✓ ✗ —

(a) ?   (b) ÷   (c) ✓   (d) ✗

3. Which cap is 7th from the left end?

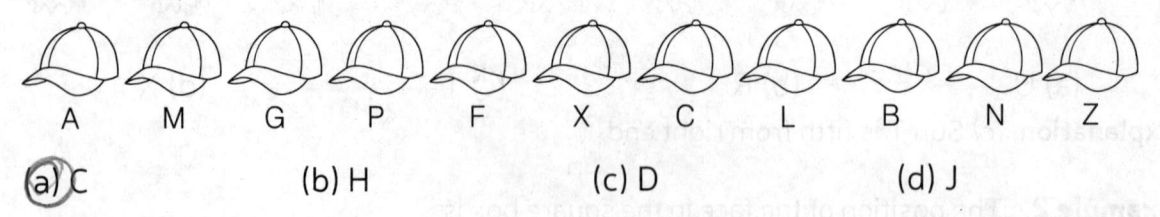

A M G P F X C L B N Z

(a) C   (b) H   (c) D   (d) J

4. Which fruit basket is 8th from the right end?

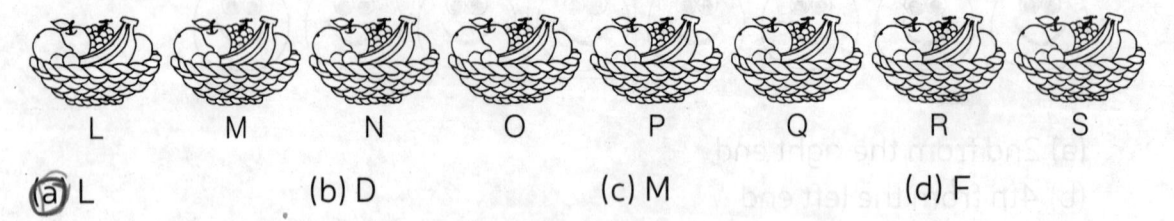

L M N O P Q R S

(a) L   (b) D   (c) M   (d) F

Direction (Q. Nos. 5-6) On the basis of following figure, fill in the blanks.

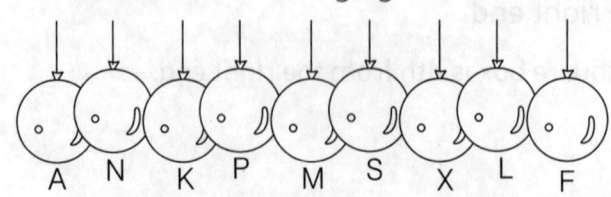

A N K P M S X L F

26   Reasoning Olympiad Class I

5. Balloon M is between _____ .

(a) balloon K and balloon X
(b) balloon P and balloon S
(c) balloon A and balloon F
(d) balloon A and balloon K

6. First balloon from the left end and first balloon from the right end are _____ .

(a) balloon A and balloon M
(b) balloon K and balloon A
(c) balloon M and balloon F
(d) balloon A and balloon F

7. The position of the circle is _____ .

□ △ ○ ◨ ⋈ × ↑ ♀ ⊥ ⋈ △

(a) 3rd from the right end
(b) 3rd from the left end
(c) 5th from the left end
(d) 5th from the right end

8. The fourth letter from the right end is _____ .

E K Z H L W B N Y

(a) T   (b) K   (c) H   (d) W

9. If there is no mango in the picture, then the apple is now the _____ item from the right end.

(a) 4th   (b) 6th
(c) 1st   (d) 3rd

Ranking Test 27

10. If there is no R in the given month, then U is now the _____ letter from the right end.

JANUARY

(a) 4th   (b) 3rd   (c) 6th   (d) 2nd

11. Subtract the 2nd number from the right end from the 5th number from the right end and you will get the _____ number from left end.

5 3 1 4 2 8

(a) 2nd   (b) 1st   (c) 4th   (d) 3rd

12. If there is no car in the picture, then the cake is now the _____ item from the left end.

(a) 3rd   (b) 4th   (c) 5th   (d) 6th

13. The position of encircled car is _____ .

(a) 1st from the right end   (b) 3rd from the left end
(c) 6th from the right end   (d) 5th from the left end

14. The second ball from the left end in the given sequence is _____ .

P   T   B   M   U   Z

(a) B   (b) T   (c) M   (d) Z

15. The position of train having 2 bogey is _____.

(a) 2nd from the left end
(b) 1st from the left end
(c) 2nd from the right end
(d) 1st from the right end

16. Which is the 4th letter from the right end in the given word?

HOLIDAYS

(a) O (b) L (c) D (d) Y

Direction (Q. Nos. 17-20) Answer the given questions on the basis of following figure.

17. Mahima is between _____.

(a) Mohan and Ramesh
(b) Pankaj and Gitika
(c) Ramesh and Gitika
(d) Pooja and Rohan

18. Who is third in the row?

(a) Pankaj (b) Mahima (c) Gitika (d) Ramesh

Ranking Test **29**

19. How many children are there in the row?

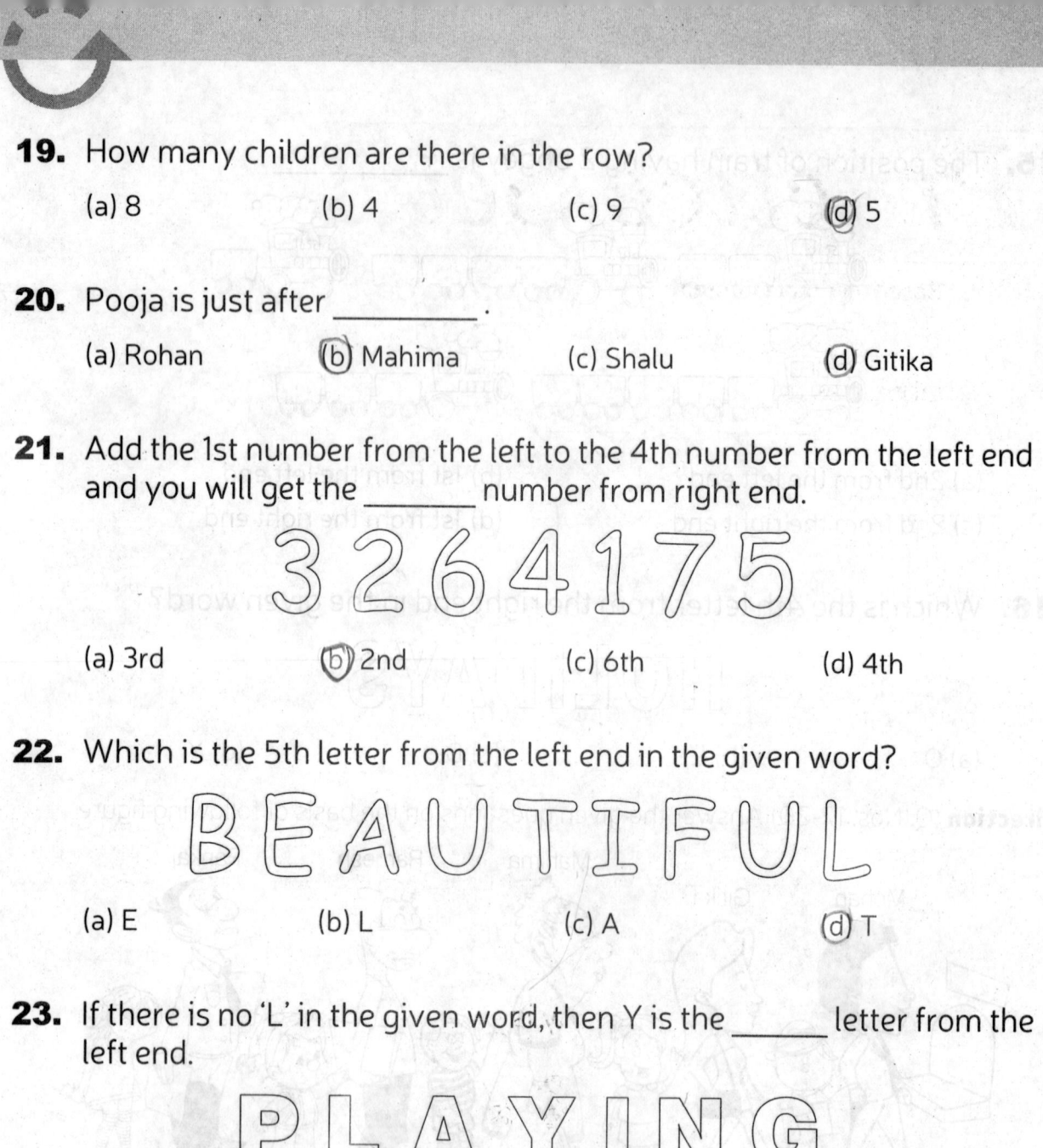

(a) 8 (b) 4 (c) 9 (d) 5

20. Pooja is just after _____.

(a) Rohan (b) Mahima (c) Shalu (d) Gitika

21. Add the 1st number from the left to the 4th number from the left end and you will get the _____ number from right end.

3 2 6 4 1 7 5

(a) 3rd (b) 2nd (c) 6th (d) 4th

22. Which is the 5th letter from the left end in the given word?

BEAUTIFUL

(a) E (b) L (c) A (d) T

23. If there is no 'L' in the given word, then Y is the _____ letter from the left end.

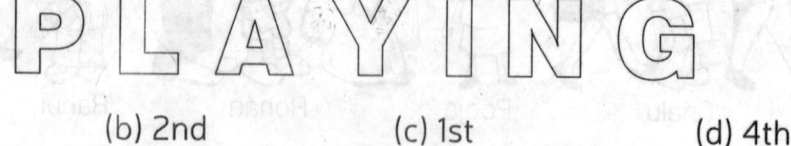

PLAYING

(a) 3rd (b) 2nd (c) 1st (d) 4th

24. Which number of the bat is fifth from the right end?

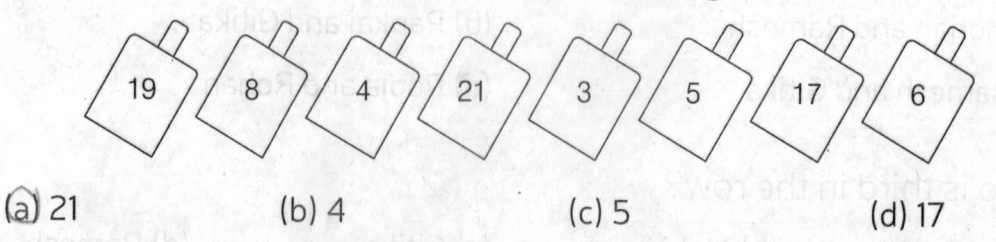

19 8 4 21 3 5 17 6

(a) 21 (b) 4 (c) 5 (d) 17

Practice Set 1

A Test Based on Whole Content

1. What comes next?

(a) (b) (c) (d)

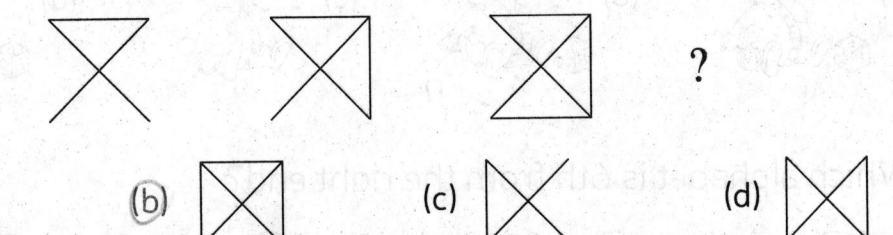

2. The given figure belongs to which group?

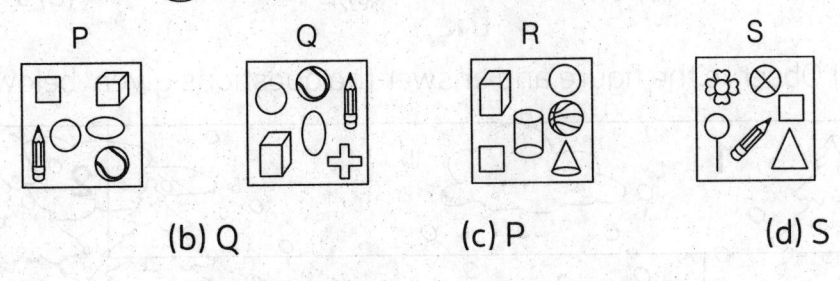

P   Q   R   S

(a) R   (b) Q   (c) P   (d) S

3. The position of car having 1 boy is _____.

(a) 3rd from the right end
(b) 4th from the right end
(c) 2nd from the left end
(d) 5th from the left end

4. In which larger shape is the shape hidden?

(a)   (b)   (c)   (d)

Practice Set 1   31

5. Which figure is exactly same as the given figure?

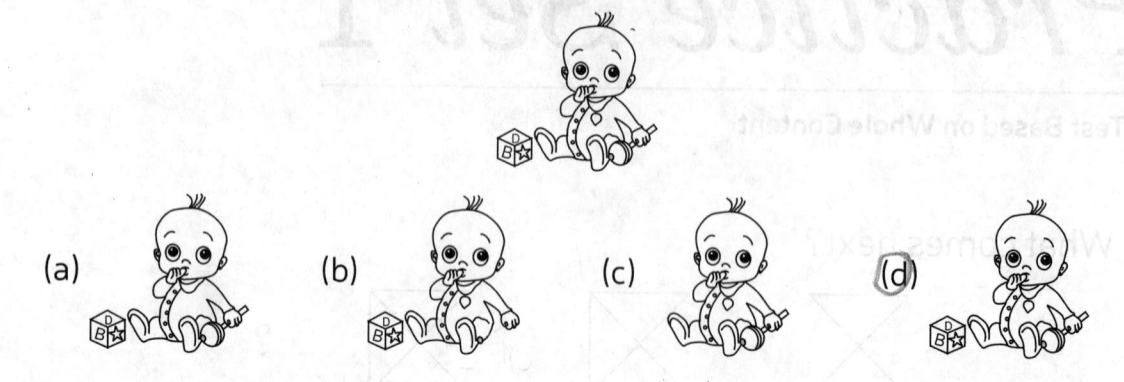

(a)　　　　(b)　　　　(c)　　　　(d)

6. Which alphabet is 6th from the right end?

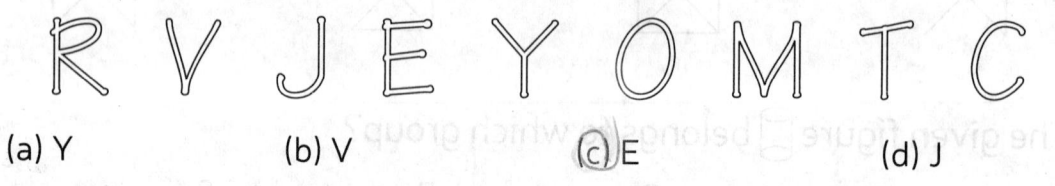

R V J E Y O M T C

(a) Y　　　　(b) V　　　　(c) E　　　　(d) J

Direction (7-9) Observe the figure and answer the questions given below.

7. In which part of the figure is the shape  hidden?

(a) 4   (b) 3   (c) 2   (d) 5

8. Which shape is hidden in part 7?

(a) 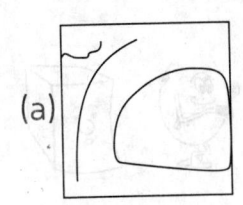   (b)    (c) 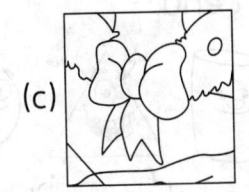   (d)

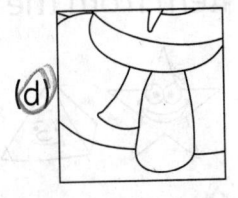

9. How many of the pictures given in the box are hidden in the part 3?

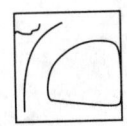

(a) 1   (b) 2   (c) 5   (d) 3

10. Which one is different from others?

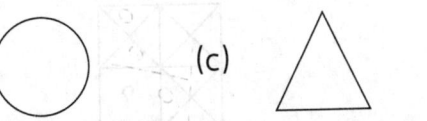

(a) 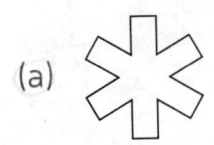   (b) 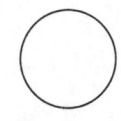   (c)   (d)

11. Which one comes next?

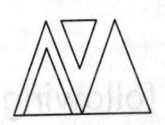

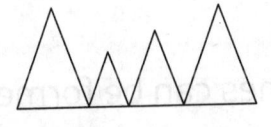

(a)    (b) 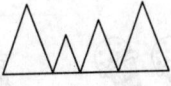   (c) 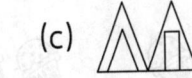   (d)

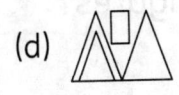

Practice Set 1 33

12. Which one is different from others?

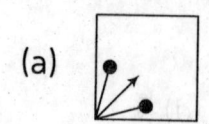

    (a)   (b) 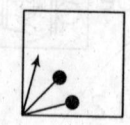   (c) 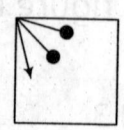   (d)

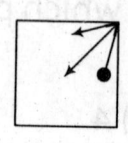

13. If there is no triangle in the given figure, then the circle is the _____ item from the left end.

    (a) 4th   (b) 6th   (c) 3rd   (d) 2nd

14. Choose the correct option.

    $D{\overset{E}{\underset{C}{}}}$: CDE :: $N{\overset{O}{\underset{M}{}}}$?

    (a) NMC   (b) MNO   (c) MXL   (d) ABC

15. Complete the following figure pattern.

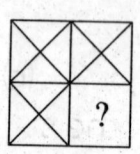

    (a) 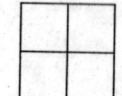   (b) 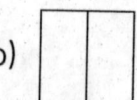   (c) 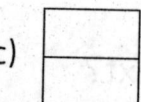   (d)

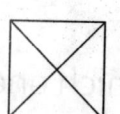

16. How many groups of 3 cones can be formed from the following figures?

    (a) 8   (b) 5   (c) 4   (d) 6

Reasoning Olympiad Class I

17. Complete the second pair in the same way as first pair.

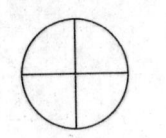

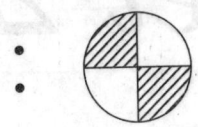

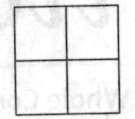

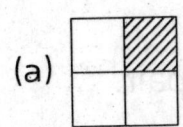

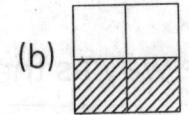

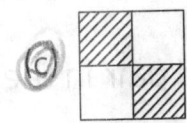

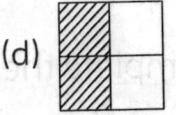

(a) (b) (c) (d)

18. Which figure is different from others?

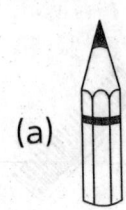

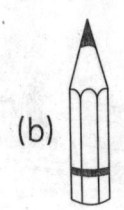

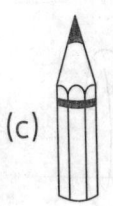

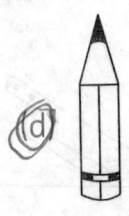

(a) (b) (c) (d)

19. Which letter is third from the left end in the word given below?

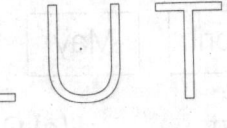

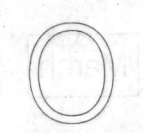

SOLUTION

(a) U (b) O (c) T (d) L

20. Complete the second pair in the same way as the first pair.

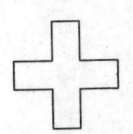

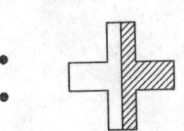

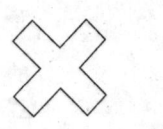

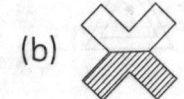

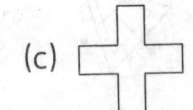

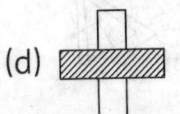

(a) (b) (c) (d)

Practice Set 1

Practice Set 2

A Test Based on the Whole Content

1. Complete the second pair in the same way as the first pair.

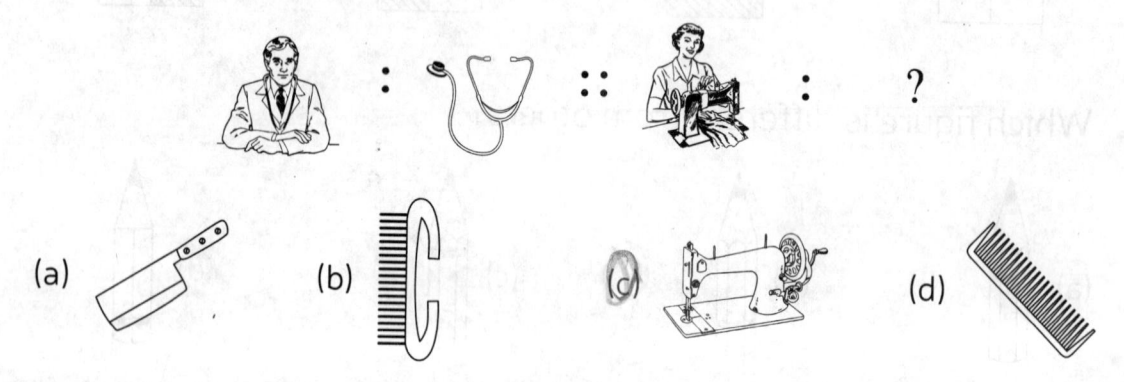

doctor :: stethoscope :: tailor : ?

(a) cleaver   (b) comb   (c) sewing machine   (d) comb

2. Which one comes next?

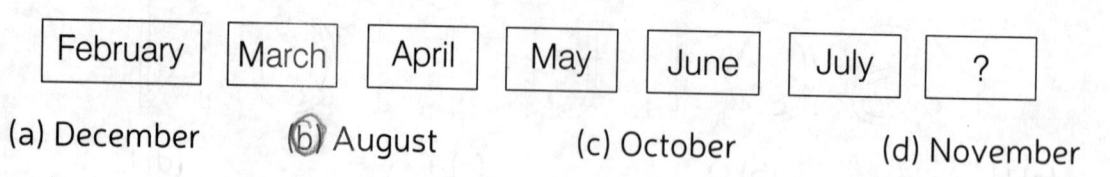

| February | March | April | May | June | July | ? |

(a) December   (b) August   (c) October   (d) November

3. Which object is same as the given figure?

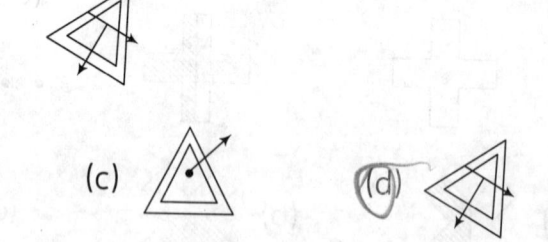

(a)   (b)   (c)   (d)

4. Which one is different from others?

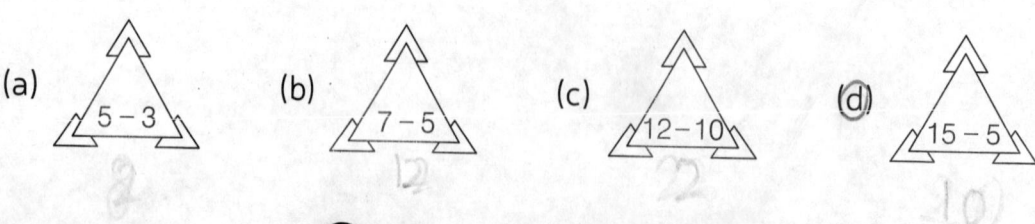

(a) 5 – 3   (b) 7 – 5   (c) 12 – 10   (d) 15 – 5

36 Reasoning Olympiad Class I

5. Find the missing figure.

(a)   (b)   (c)   (d)

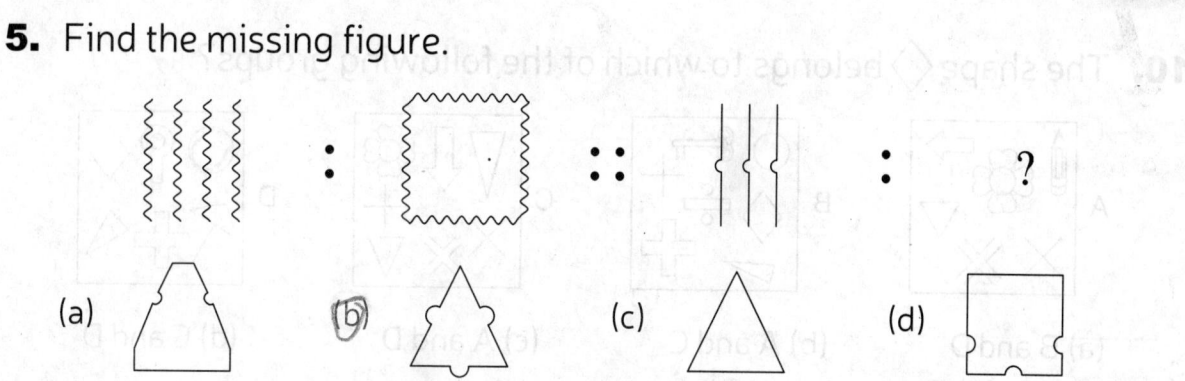

Direction (6-8) Fill in the blanks on the basis of given figure.

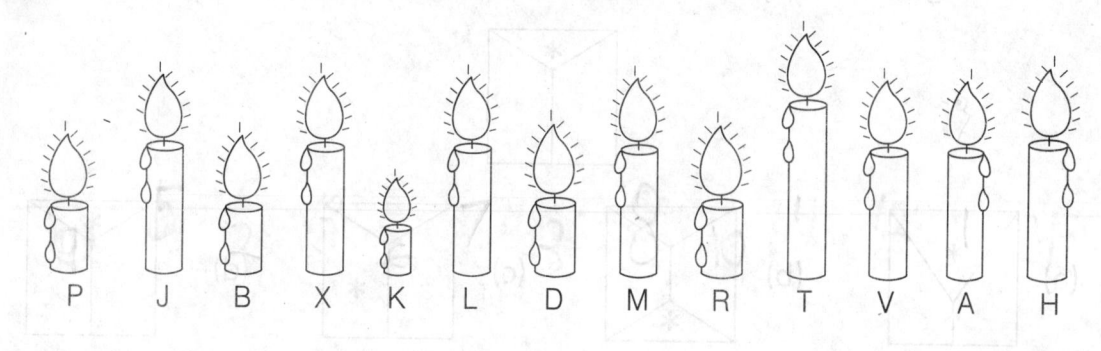

P   J   B   X   K   L   D   M   R   T   V   A   H

6. Candle K is between _____.

(a) candle J and candle D (b) candle R and candle V
(c) candle X and candle L (d) candle B and candle L

7. The position of shortest candle is _____.

(a) 5th from the right end (b) 5th from the left end
(c) 7th from the left end   (d) 7th from the right end

8. The shortest and longest candle are _____.

(a) K and A   (b) M and B   (c) K and T   (d) H and K

9. Which one comes next?

0 4   0 6   0 8   1 0   ?

(a) 1 2   (b) 1 2   (c) 1 4   (d) 1 4

Practice Set 2   37

10. The shape ◇ belongs to which of the following groups?

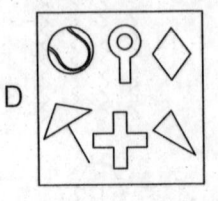

(a) B and D   (b) A and C   (c) A and D   (d) C and D

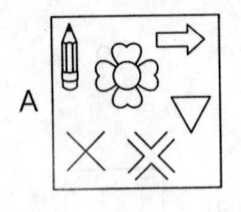

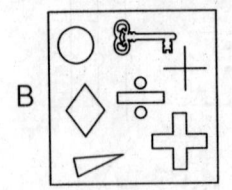

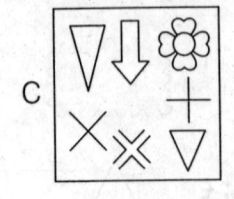

11. Which figure is same as the given figure?

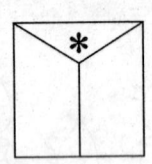

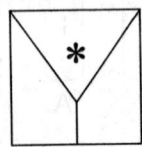

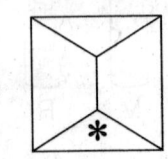

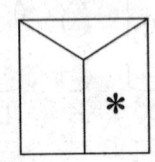

12. Find the other half of the picture given below.

13. Find the missing figure.

U S N : ☀ :: T H A : ?

(a) 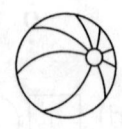   (b)    (c)    (d)

14. The position of number in the circle is _____.

4 1 8 2 ⑤ 6 3 7

(a) 1st from the right end (b) 3rd from the left end
(c) 6th from the right end (d) 5th from the left end

15. The position △ from the right end is _____.

○ □ ⬠ ◇ ⬡ △ ◯ ⊠ $ ⌂ ✕

(a) 5th (b) 4th (c) 6th (d) 3rd

16. Which one comes next?

ABC   DEF   ?   JKL   MNO

(a) AZB   (b) MKL   (c) GHI   (d) RBF

17. In which larger shape is the shape 🎀 hidden?

(a)   (b)   (c)   (d)

Practice Set 2   39

18. Which one is different from others?

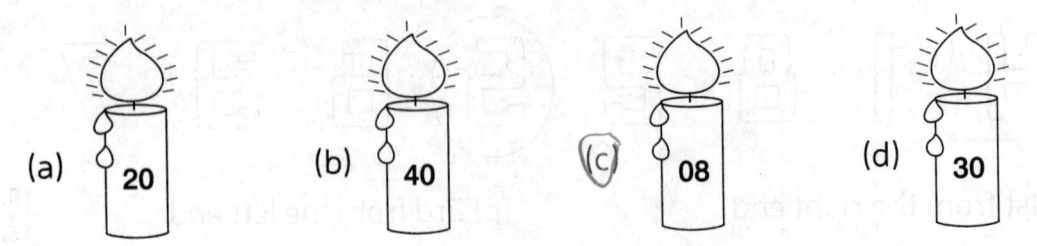

(a) 20 (b) 40 (c) 08 (d) 30

19. Which option will replace the question mark?

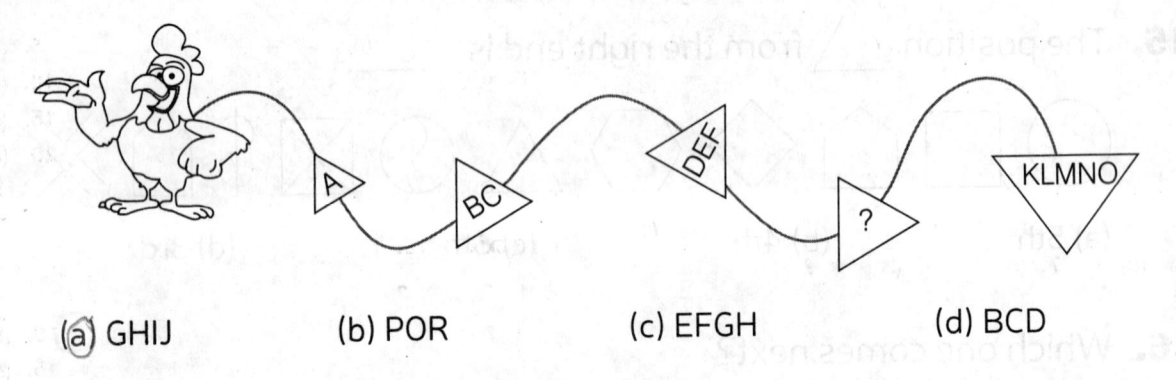

A → BC → DEF → ? → KLMNO

(a) GHIJ (b) POR (c) EFGH (d) BCD

20. Choose the figure which will complete the given figure pattern.

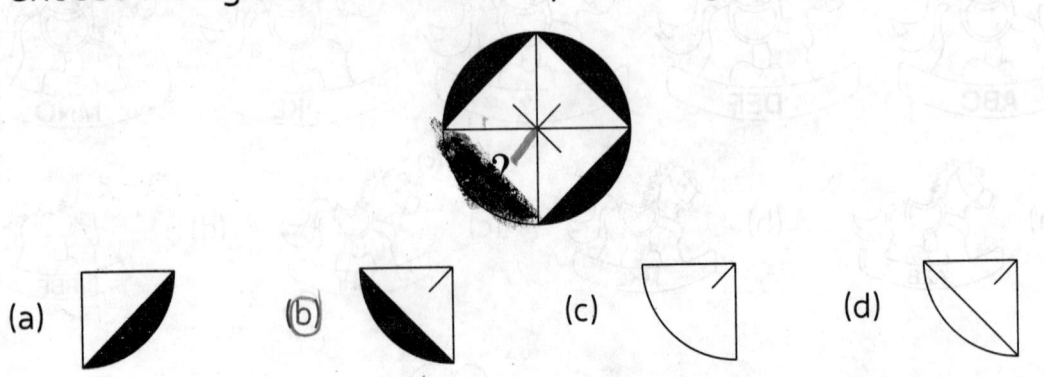

(a) (b) (c) (d)

Answers

Chapter 1 : Matching Pairs

1. (c)	2. (c)	3. (a)	4. (b)	5. (a)
6. (d)	7. (b)	8. (c)	9. (c)	10. (b)
11. (b)	12. (b)	13. (a)	14. (a)	15. (c)
16. (d)	17. (d)	18. (a)	19. (d)	20. (c)
21. (d)	22. (a)	23. (c)	24. (a)	

Chapter 2 : Which One is Different?

1. (a)	2. (c)	3. (c)	4. (d)	5. (d)
6. (b)	7. (b)	8. (c)	9. (b)	10. (b)
11. (d)	12. (c)	13. (b)	14. (c)	15. (c)
16. (b)	17. (c)	18. (c)	19. (a)	20. (d)

Chapter 3 : What Comes Next?

1. (c)	2. (d)	3. (c)	4. (d)	5. (b)
6. (c)	7. (c)	8. (b)	9. (b)	10. (c)
11. (b)	12. (c)	13. (d)	14. (b)	15. (c)
16. (c)	17. (b)	18. (c)	19. (b)	

Chapter 4 : Similar Shapes and Grouping of Figures

1. (c)	2. (d)	3. (c)	4. (c)	5. (d)
6. (c)	7. (d)	8. (c)	9. (c)	10. (b)
11. (b)	12. (b)	13. (c)	14. (a)	15. (d)
16. (b)	17. (c)	18. (b)	19. (b)	20. (a)
21. (d)				

Chapter 5 : Hidden Shapes and Pattern Completion

1. (a)	2. (b)	3. (d)	4. (b)	5. (b)
6. (b)	7. (c)	8. (d)	9. (d)	10. (c)
11. (b)	12. (a)	13. (c)	14. (c)	15. (c)
16. (c)	17. (a)	18. (c)	19. (b)	20. (a)
21. (c)	22. (d)			

Chapter 6 : Ranking Test

1. (c)	2. (c)	3. (a)	4. (a)	5. (b)
6. (d)	7. (b)	8. (d)	9. (c)	10. (b)
11. (d)	12. (a)	13. (d)	14. (b)	15. (b)
16. (c)	17. (d)	18. (c)	19. (d)	20. (d)
21. (b)	22. (d)	23. (a)	24. (a)	

Practice Set 1

1. (b)	2. (a)	3. (b)	4. (d)	5. (d)
6. (c)	7. (d)	8. (d)	9. (b)	10. (b)
11. (b)	12. (d)	13. (a)	14. (b)	15. (d)
16. (d)	17. (c)	18. (d)	19. (d)	20. (a)

Practice Set 2

1. (c)	2. (b)	3. (d)	4. (d)	5. (b)
6. (c)	7. (b)	8. (c)	9. (b)	10. (a)
11. (d)	12. (b)	13. (d)	14. (d)	15. (c)
16. (c)	17. (a)	18. (c)	19. (a)	20. (b)

Answers and Explanations

Chapter 1 : Matching Pairs

1. *(c)* Bag is used to put the books. Similarly, flower pot is used to put the flowers.
2. *(c)* Dots are connected with lines to form a geometrical shape.
3. *(a)* + or × of first figure will disappear to get second figure.
4. *(b)* Given lines are use to form the second figure.
5. *(a)* Black area interchanges with white area.
6. *(d)* Letters are arranged in alphabetical order.
7. *(b)* White area of the figure becomes gray.
8. *(c)* Second figure is the completed figure of the first figure.
9. *(c)* Number of objects is equal to the number of the lines in second figure.
10. *(b)* × or + disappears and the remaining elements are arranged in the square shape.
11. *(b)* First figure is divided into two parts to form the second figure.
12. *(b)* Inner shape becomes the outer shape and outer shape becomes the inner shape.
13. *(a)* First figure is formed from the second figure.
14. *(a)* Second figure completes the first figure.
15. *(c)* Shaded portion becomes unshaded and unshaded portion becomes shaded.
16. *(d)* Single shape turns into double shapes and double shapes turns into single shape.
17. *(d)* Second figure is the part of the first figure.
18. *(a)* Second figure is the remaining right half of the first figure.
19. *(d)* Number of *zig-zag* lines is increased by two in second figure.
20. *(c)* Outer small shapes become central shape and central shape becomes outer shapes.
21. *(d)* Plane and bird fly in the sky. Similarly, ship and duck swims in the water.
22. *(a)* Second figure is the top view of the first figure.
23. *(c)* Second figure is the mirror reflection of the first figure.
24. *(a)* Combination of letters in first figure is the name of the second figure.

Chapter 2 : Which One is Different?

1. *(a)* Except option (a), all are vegetables.
2. *(c)* All options have 7 triangles except option (c).
3. *(c)* Except figure (c), all other figures have straight lines.
4. *(d)* Except option (d), all other months have 31 days.
5. *(d)* In all other figures except figure (d), the inner and outer shapes are same.
6. *(b)* Except option (b), the base of arrow is same.
7. *(b)* Except option (b), there are only two bottom lines.
8. *(c)* Except option (c), there are two circles and one triangle in all other options.
9. *(b)* The arrow is pointing upward, except in option (b).
10. *(b)* All objects are used for cutting, except option (b).
11. *(d)* All objects are the source of light, except option (d).
12. *(c)* Except option (c), designs of options (a), (b) and (d) are made by straight lines.
13. *(b)* All figures have both the hands in same direction except figure (b).
14. *(c)* All options have same addition of numbers i.e. 5, except option (c).
15. *(c)* Except option (c), all other options have two similar shapes.
16. *(b)* Except figure (b), the black circle is placed at the edge of large circle.
17. *(c)* Except option (c), all trees have flowers.
18. *(c)* Except option (c), all have five leaves.

19. (a) Except option (a), numbers of lines inside the figure is equal to the sides of the figure drawn.

20. (d) Except option (d), drawn circles of the lines are facing in opposite direction.

Chapter 3 : What Comes Next?

1. (c) In every new figure, one new line appears.
2. (d) After third figure, pattern is repeated. So, second figure will be next figure.
3. (c) Number of cartoons decreased by 2 in every next figure.
4. (d) The letters are given in backward order.
5. (b) First and second figures are opposite to each other, third and fourth figure opposite to each other. Similarly, sixth figure will be opposite of fifth figure.
6. (c) Each time the circle and the square is increased by one.
7. (c) Each time the small square moves one block forward.
8. (b) Sequence shows alternate names of the months.
9. (b) After third figure, series is repeated.
10. (c) Each time one circle is added.
11. (b) Small square shifts one step downward in each step.
12. (c) Each time number is decreased by 3.
13. (d) A new line is added in each step.
14. (b) Each object changes its position from vertical to horizontal direction.
15. (c) A new line is added in each step.
16. (c) After third figure, pattern is repeated.
17. (b) After second figure, outer shape is repeated and one triangle is added in every step.
18. (d) Last letter is repeated two times in figure A i.e. K.
19. (b) Numbers in A are multiple of 3 and numbers in C are multiple of 1. Similarly, numbers in B are multiple of 2.

Chapter 4 : Similar Shapes and Grouping of Figures

1. (c) Triangle is present in the given group.
2. (d) Option (d) is present in given group of toy.
3. (c) Smiley of option (c) belongs to the given group.
4. (c) The given figure ☐ belongs to the group (c).
5. (d) Option (d) is exactly same as the given figure.
6. (c) Option (c) is exactly same as the given figure.
7. (d) Option (d) is exactly same as the given figure.
8. (c) Option (c) is exactly same as the given figure.
9. (c) Option (c) is exactly same as the given figure.
10. (b) Option (b) is exactly same as the given figure.
11. (c) Option (c) is exactly same as the given figure.
12. (b) Option (b) is exactly same as the given figure.
13. (c) Option (c) is exactly same as the given figure.
14. (a) Option (a) is exactly same as the given figure.
15. (d) Option (d) is exactly same as the given figure.
16. (b) Option (b) is exactly same as the given figure.
17. (c)
18. (b)
19. (b) There are 4 group of 6 straws.
20. (a) 15 hexagons are present in the given figure. So, there are 5 groups of 3 hexagon.
21. (d) The shapes in figures A and B are different from each other by shape and size.

Chapter 5 : Hidden Shapes and Pattern Completion

1. (a) Shape of option (a) is hidden in part 3.
2. (b) The shape given in the question is hidden in part 7.
3. (d) Two pictures are hidden in part 7.
4. (b) There are 10 eyes in part 4.
5. (b) The shape given in the question is hidden in part 6.
6. (b) Shape of option (b) is hidden in part 3.
7. (c) There are 2 stands in part 7.
8. (d) The given shape is hidden in option (d).
9. (d) The given shape is hidden in option (d).
10. (c) The given shape is hidden in option (c).
11. (b) The given shape is hidden in option (b).
12. (a) The given shape is hidden in option (a).
13. (c) The given shape is hidden in option (c).
14. (c) Figure (c) exactly matches the question figure.
15. (c) Figure (c) exactly matches the question figure.
16. (c) Figure (c) completes the given picture.
17. (a) Figure (a) exactly matches the question figure.
18. (c) Figure (c) exactly matches the question figure.
19. (b) Figure (b) completes the given figure pattern.
20. (a) Figure (a) completes the given figure pattern.
21. (c) Figure (c) completes the given figure pattern.
22. (d) Figure (d) completes the given figure pattern.

Chapter 6 : Ranking Test

1. (c) Monkey A is fifth from the left end.
2. (c) Image in option (c) is 3rd from the right end.
3. (a) Cap C is 7th from the left end.
4. (a) Fruit basket L is 8th from the right end.
5. (b) Balloon M is between balloon P and balloon S.
6. (d) First balloon from the left end and first balloon from the right end are balloon A and balloon F.
7. (b) The position of the circle is 3rd from the left end.
8. (d) W is the fourth letter from the right end.
9. (c) When there is no mango in the given figure, then the apple is the 1st item from the right end.
10. (b) If there is no R in the given month, then U is the 3rd letter from the right end.
11. (d) 5th number from the right end is 3 and 2nd number from the right end is 2, then 3 – 2 = 1. So, 1 is the 3rd number from the left end.
12. (a) If there is no car in the given picture, then the cake is now the 3rd item from the left end.
13. (d) The position of car in circle is 5th from the left end.
14. (b) The second ball from the left end is T.
15. (b) The position of train having 2 bogey is 1st from the left end.
16. (c) Letter D is the 4th letter from the right end in the given word.
17. (d) Mahima is between Pooja and Rohan.
18. (c) Gitika is third in the given row.
19. (d) There are 5 children in the given row.
20. (d) Pooja is just after Gitika.
21. (b) 1st number from the left end is 3 and 4th number from the left end is 4, then 3 + 4 = 7. So, 7 is 2nd from the right end.
22. (d) Letter T is the 5th letter from the left end in the given word.
23. (a) If there is no 'L' in the given word, then Y is the 3rd letter from the left end.
24. (a) Bat having number 21 is at the fifth position from the right end.

Reasoning Olympiad Class I